THE
MAKING OF AMERICA
SERIES

SANTA MONICA
A HISTORY ON THE EDGE

With the opening of the Santa Monica Pleasure Pier (also known as the Looff Pier) in 1916, Santa Monica's leisure industry got a boost. The Hippodrome, built to house a carousel, still stands today. The electric tram on the walkway ferried passengers between Ocean Park and the Pleasure Pier. (Courtesy of the Santa Monica Public Library Image Archives, Elizabeth R. Sedat Collection.)

THE
MAKING OF AMERICA
SERIES

SANTA MONICA
A HISTORY ON THE EDGE

PAULA A. SCOTT

ARCADIA
PUBLISHING

Copyright © 2004 by Paula A. Scott
ISBN 978-0-7385-2469-6

Published by Arcadia Publishing
Charleston, South Carolina

Printed in the United States of America

Library of Congress Catalog Card Number: 2004109614

For all general information contact Arcadia Publishing at:
Telephone 843-853-2070
Fax 843-853-0044
E-Mail sales@arcadiapublishing.com
For customer service and orders:
Toll-Free 1-888-313-2665

Visit us on the Internet at www.arcadiapublishing.com

CONTENTS

ACKNOWLEDGMENTS

I have benefited from the help of many people and institutions during the writing of this book and am pleased to have a chance to say thank you. The Santa Monica Public Library was an invaluable resource in researching this book. The public library's skilled reference librarians answered innumerable questions and provided helpful suggestions on diverse topics. I am particularly grateful to Cynni Murphy, supervisor of the image archives at the public library, for her help in obtaining historic photographs for the book. Thanks also to the Santa Monica Historical Society for allowing me access to some of their rich holdings, and to the Getty Research Institute for assistance with their collection of historic images. I am grateful to Mr. Lloyd Allen, who generously consented to be interviewed and shared his recollections of Santa Monica's African-American community with me. Professor Darrell Goode of Santa Monica College also contributed information on the subject as did Professor Doug Flamming of the Georgia Institute of Technology. I would like to thank Harold Zinkin for permission to use photographs from Muscle Beach and Harold Osmer and Phil Harms for the use of photos from the Santa Monica road races. I am grateful to Pat Samarge of Franklin Elementary School and Dan Dawson of Santa Monica's Big Blue Bus for kindly sharing historic images with me as well. My appreciation goes to Naomi Lamoreaux and David Lappen, both of whom offered technical help in scanning material. Several people read drafts of the manuscript and made valuable comments. Many thanks to Susan Giesberg, Daniel Bleiberg, Susan Richey, and Jean-Laurent Rosenthal for their time, energy, and thoughtful readings. Arcadia editors Jim Kempert and Rob Kangas have been helpful every step of the way. I am grateful for their encouragement and advice. Finally, I wish to thank Manuel, Isabelle, and Juliette Rosenthal for their support as the book was being written.

INTRODUCTION

Santa Monica, California is more than just a small city of local renown. It is a place whose name resonates widely, a place where trends begin, a place of interest disproportionate to its modest size. Located in Southern California, it has, like the region itself, caught the fancy of generations of people who moved westward, or dreamt of moving westward, to an almost mythical land of health, wealth, and sunshine. Located at the endpoint of two important routes west—Route 66 and Interstate 10—Santa Monica has been a destination for tourists and immigrants alike and appeared in the consciousness of many others as someplace special, even if they never made the trip. This reputation has been strengthened and enhanced by Santa Monica's long association with numerous nationally-known celebrities and public figures, from Collis Huntington, the great nineteenth-century railroad magnate, to scores of movie-star residents including Shirley Temple, Bette Davis, Clark Gable, Robert Redford, and Jane Fonda, to actor-turned-politician Arnold Schwartzenegger, who lived here during his bachelor days and recently ran his campaign for governor in the 2003 recall election from his office complex on Main Street. Besides famous residents, the city has repeatedly been in the spotlight for the many remarkable things that have happened here. Nationally-watched automobile races, historic airplane flights, a part in countless films and television shows, roles in novels by writers such as Raymond Chandler, attention-getting politics, and contributions to leisure culture in tennis, bodybuilding, and skateboarding, have all helped secure for Santa Monica a compelling history.

But the story of Santa Monica is not only interesting for the people and events that have repeatedly catapulted it into the nation's consciousness. Santa Monica is a place worth knowing for its local stories. From pristine open land traversed only by native Gabrielino Indians, to a backwater in Spain's far flung New World empire, to ranchos under Mexican rule, to a boomtown powered by real-estate speculation, to the mature city of the 2000s, Santa Monica has seen a lot. All along, the many diverse peoples who have made Santa Monica home have each contributed stories that enliven the tale. The city has seen good times and bad and participated, in its own unique way, in the great historical events and movements of the last several hundred years and, all the while, grown up side by side with and adapted to the enormous and sometimes overpowering metropolis called Los Angeles.

Santa Monica's history has been lived on the edge in many different senses: on the edge of the North American continent, on the edge of the Pacific Ocean, on the edge of empire, on the edge of Los Angeles, on the edge of greatness, occasionally even on the edge of ruin, and always very much on the cutting edge. Here is the story of this extraordinary place.

Chapter One

ORIGINS: NATIVE PEOPLES

OF THE SANTA MONICA AREA

Santa Monica today is a city of 86,000 people, bounded on three sides by Los Angeles and by the Pacific Ocean on the fourth. Its official elevation is 101 feet above sea level, but until relatively recently, at least in geological time, the area that now forms the city was submerged under the sea. Indeed, about a million years ago Santa Monica was a bay, not a beach town. The current shape of the city, with high cliffs overlooking the beach, was formed as the sea subsided and sand and gravel was subsequently swept down the Santa Monica Mountains towards the ocean by the natural forces of erosion. Over time, these materials formed an apron of deposits that spread out past the current shoreline. As the sea advanced again and the shoreline shifted, waves began to eat away at this apron of alluvial material, cutting deeply into it to form today's ocean-facing palisades.

It was not until more than 10,000 years ago that humans arrived in the area. These first residents of the Los Angeles Basin were part of a great migration of people who originally came from Asia via the land bridges over the Bering Strait that once connected Siberia to Alaska. Traversing Alaska and Canada by way of an ice-free corridor, these people eventually made their way to Southern California. These first Southern Californians were Hokan-speaking hunters who found plentiful game in the birds, deer, horses, bison, and other now-extinct animals thriving here in the Los Angeles Basin. Over millennia the lifeways of these early peoples changed as coastal Southern Californians began to depend less on hunting and more on plant foods for their survival. We know, for example, that by around 6000 B.C. native peoples were grinding the wild seeds they collected using milling stones and that their diet was more diverse due to the increasing use of plant foods.

Material evidence of their many centuries of life in the area has been found at locations including Rancho La Brea and at Malaga Cove, near present-day Palos Verdes, where stone tools were found. A young woman's skeletal remains, dating back approximately 8,000 years, were found in the La Brea Tar Pits excavations and, more recently, 7,000-year-old skeletons were unearthed when a trailer park was being built in Malibu in 1969. We know from archeological remains that these early Southern Californians also colonized the offshore islands and possessed seafaring skills that allowed for human habitation of San Clemente Island by 7785 B.C. and San Nicolas Island by 6210 B.C.

Life in prehistoric California was far from static. Just as new migrations would change the face of modern California, ancient migrations altered the lives of

Californians thousands of years ago. Indeed, major change came to the Los Angeles area sometime between 2000 B.C. and 700 A.D. with the arrival of a very different people from the Great Basin area hundreds of miles to the northeast. The precise moment when this migration took place is disputed. It is quite possible it occurred over a long period of time rather than suddenly. In either case, the arrival of these new Uto-Aztecans (so-called because they spoke a language belonging to the Uto-Aztecan, also known as Shoshonean, linguistic stock) transformed life in the Los Angeles–Santa Monica Bay area.

No one knows what drove these Uto-Aztecans from the Great Basin westward, but we do know that over time they became widely dispersed throughout Southern California and eventually came to dominate the region, either by absorbing or by pushing aside the Hokan peoples who had lived here for many centuries. (Although Hokan speakers did continue to persist in some areas—the Chumash of the Santa Barbara area are a prominent example.) Once dispersed throughout Southern California, it was only a matter of time before different regional subcultures developed among the Uto-Aztecans. As a result, by the time of first contact with Europeans in the sixteenth century, a number of linguistically and culturally distinctive groups existed in Southern California, each with its own well-established territory.

Of all these groups, only one is central to Santa Monica's story—that of the Gabrielinos (also called Tongva). So named because of their later association with Mission San Gabriel, the Gabrielinos were one of the richest and most culturally sophisticated native societies in California. (The Native Americans known as Fernandeños because of their links to Mission San Fernando were essentially Gabrielinos as well, and are included in the general description that follows.) Claiming the Santa Monica area as their domain, as well as most of present-day Los Angeles and Orange Counties, the Gabrielinos were estimated to number about 5,000 in 1770. They were a hunting and gathering society whose cultural influence extended well past their boundaries to surrounding tribes.

The land that makes up the city of Santa Monica today fell close to the western boundary of Gabrielino territory. Somewhere between Malibu Creek and Topanga Creek was the line of division between the Hokan-speaking Chumash, whose territory extended up past present-day Santa Barbara, and the Gabrielino, whose territory reached all the way to the foot of the San Gabriel Mountains in the north, to the vicinity of San Bernardino in the east, to the Newport Beach/Laguna Beach area down the coast, and out to sea to include the offshore islands of San Clemente, Santa Catalina, and San Nicolas.

It has been estimated that the Gabrielino were settled into about fifty villages throughout this large territory around the time Europeans first colonized the area. It is quite likely that at some time the Gabrielino maintained settlements in present-day Santa Monica. As Dolan Eargle, an authority on California Indians, has written, "there is probably not a flat, a marsh, or a valley in the state that did not once support a native village."[1] Certainly the Gabrielino were well acquainted with the Santa Monica area. William McCawley, a Gabrielino expert, reports that the Gabrielino had specific names to refer to Santa Monica—one Gabrielino informant reported the name Kecheekvet and another mentioned Koruuvanga. Unfortunately, we will never know the locations of many Gabrielino villages, in Santa Monica or elsewhere, because by the 1860s those who had had sure knowledge of such settlements had already taken it with them to their graves.

Villages not far from today's Santa Monica have been pinpointed. Only about six miles west from central Santa Monica, as the crow flies, was the community of Topaa'nga in Topanga Canyon, where a large cemetery once attested to the many Gabrielinos who had lived there. In the 1930s when Pacific Coast Highway was being widened some evidence of a village was unearthed at the mouth of Santa Monica Canyon. Unfortunately, a proper study of the site was not conducted and not much is known about its age or composition. There is better evidence for a significant community to the southeast, called Saa'anga, near Ballona Creek. Another community, Waachnga, was likely also in the vicinity of Ballona Creek. When Spanish explorers led by Portolá came through the Los Angeles area in 1769, they stopped not far from today's Veterans Administration complex on Wilshire Boulevard. Here they reported finding "a good village" of native people. (This may have been the place called Koruuvanga mentioned above.) If villages have not been documented in Santa Monica itself, it is clear that the area was well known to the Gabrielinos and that nearby lands were definitely settled.

The Santa Monica/Los Angeles area was blessed then, as now, with a pleasant climate that made life easier for the native inhabitants compared to those living in the desert or mountain regions of California. Adapted to this climate, Gabrielino villages consisted of relatively lightweight structures made with upright poles arranged in a circle and bent inward to meet at the center of the roof. These poles were then covered with tule reeds—a type of bulrush native to California—or ferns. In Southern California's mild climate, clothing could also be spare. Women typically wore aprons made of animal skin, tule, bark, or other plant fibers. Meanwhile men and children wore nothing at all, except in colder weather. Then men, women, and children donned capes or cloaks fashioned of animal skins or rabbit fur. As adornment, both sexes wore ear ornaments in pierced ears and shell beads strung into necklaces and bracelets. Women and children wore fresh flowers as well, when they were available. The Gabrielino also marked themselves with tattoos on their faces and bodies and wore body paint or ochre on some occasions.

Just as the climate made living relatively comfortable for the Gabrielino, so did access to a wide variety of foods. Situated on the coast, the Gabrielinos of the Santa Monica Bay area profited from the abundance of the sea with fish (including large species such as tuna and shark), shellfish such as abalone and limpets, sea birds, and marine mammals contributing to their diet. Because the Gabrielino were proficient seafarers, both with canoes and rafts, and had developed effective tools such as harpoons and nets, the bounty of the sea was well within their reach. On land the

Gabrielino were skillful hunters, employing bows and arrows, traps, slings, and throwing sticks to catch game such as deer, coyote, rabbits, birds, snakes, and rats.

Though not an agricultural people, the Gabrielino enriched their diet by exploiting plant resources, especially acorns. Used throughout California by native peoples, acorns are quite nourishing and, prepared as mush, constituted a staple of Gabrielino cuisine. Though today chia seeds are mostly a novelty, the Gabrielinos knew chia to be a useful plant yielding both seeds and shoots. Gabrielino Indians also gathered various roots and bulbs that their long experience with the wild plants of Southern California had proved to be healthful.

The Gabrielino economy was anchored not only on what was available locally, but what could be obtained through trade as well. Evidence of trading between Gabrielinos and inland groups exists from as early as 900–1000 A.D. Products from the islands, especially items made of soapstone, were brought to the mainland where the Gabrielino sometimes traded them inland, along with valuable items such as shell beads, dried fish, and sea otter pelts. In exchange the Gabrielino obtained animal skins, seeds, acorns, obsidian, and other useful items not available locally. Well located between the islands and inland tribes, the coastal Gabrielino profited from a significant trade network extending hundreds of miles inland so that, even in the days before any modern transportation, shells and soapstone originating with the Gabrielino could be found in service among people as far away as the Pueblo Indians of New Mexico.

Thanks to trade, the natural productivity of their territory, and their prowess at hunting and gathering, the Gabrielino were a wealthy people. But the richness of Gabrielino culture was not just material. These southern Californians developed a religious system that infused their lives with spiritual significance. While there is much confusion today about the origins and practice of much Gabrielino religion, some have suggested that the Gabrielino were religious innovators whose ideas and rituals influenced the practices of their non-Gabrielino neighbors. In addition, surviving examples of the beautiful baskets, objects inlaid with shells, finely-crafted tools, and rock art made by the Gabrielino testify to the vibrant and creative culture that once flourished here.

Though this much is known about the Gabrielino, our understanding of this once dominant and flourishing people will always be tragically limited. By the time anthropologists and ethnologists began serious study of native southern Californians, knowledgeable Gabrielino sources had disappeared and the culture itself had largely disintegrated under the weight of Spanish, Mexican, and then American dominance. Physical evidence of their long residence in the Santa Monica and Los Angeles area has mostly vanished as well. Between casual souvenir hunters, who pocketed artifacts by the hundreds, and the bulldozers that remade ancient Gabrielino sites into booming cities, much was lost. In fact, only a small fraction of the archaeological sites that might have shed light on the Gabrielinos have been preserved and properly investigated.

Origins: Native Peoples of the Santa Monica Area

Our knowledge of their history is incomplete, but their significance to the area is indisputable. As residents of the land for millennia—far longer than their conquerors have lived here—Santa Monica was theirs for centuries before Europeans even dreamed of California. While it is often assumed that the Gabrielino are now an extinct people, they have persisted to the present and continue to add a unique element to the ethnic tapestry of Southern California. Indeed, in October of 2003 descendants of the Gabrielino met at the former site of the "good village" near University High School for a Native-American arts and crafts festival. Gabrielino Indians also meet at Mission San Gabriel every September for a festival, and it is estimated that 400 to 500 Gabrielino descendants currently reside in the San Gabriel Valley. Moreover, it was the Gabrielinos, through their labor, who would make the first European development of the region by the Spanish possible. Then, under Mexican rule they would continue to do the backbreaking toil involved in working the land, not only in Santa Monica but across California. These contributions, which highlighted the region's vast agricultural potential, attracted others here and helped set in motion the modern settlement of California. Unfortunately, these unfolding events would also be the engine of decline for the once-flourishing Gabrielinos.

Chapter Two

UNDER SPANISH RULE

Events unfolding on the other side of the world in Europe would dramatically disrupt the ways of the Santa Monica area's Gabrielinos and alter the region indelibly. International rivalries among powers such as Spain, England, and Russia sent repercussions throughout the New World as these nations sought to develop and exploit new lands to their own advantage. Initially, however, change came slowly. Spain explored the coast of what is today the state of California, or *Alta California* as they knew it, and claimed Santa Monica, along with the rest of the region, in the sixteenth century. Spain then proceeded to ignore Alta California for about two centuries. Then, fearing competition from its rivals, Spain finally began a colonization program that brought the region's Native Americans, including the coastal Gabrielino, under the control of a string of Franciscan missions. This new approach meant dramatic change for Alta California's native peoples. Unfortunately, the inhabitants of the Santa Monica area would never fully recover from their encounter with this alien civilization. Meanwhile, the Santa Monica area itself was transformed from an age-old Gabrielino territory into a remote backwater in Spain's far flung New World empire. Santa Monica played only a peripheral role in Spain's Alta California plans, but it too was irreversibly changed by Spanish rule.

Spaniards were the first Europeans to see the Santa Monica Bay area. The period between 1513 and 1543 was a time of feverish exploration as Iberian adventurers, inspired by stories of treasures and cities built of gold, fanned out across much of the southern part of today's United States seeking fortunes for themselves and for the king of Spain. Juan Rodríguez Cabrillo—leader of the first exploration of the California coast in 1542—was one such explorer. Though born in Europe, Cabrillo had spent most of his life in the New World and was, by the time of his California voyage, a veteran of the Spanish conquests of Cuba, Mexico, Guatemala, and Honduras. Offered the opportunity to explore the California coast by ship, Cabrillo prepared three vessels and departed from Mexico with two goals. First, he wanted to locate the western end of a strait that was thought, erroneously it turned out, to bisect North America. Second, he hoped to find rich civilizations such as the ones the Spanish were already profiting from in Mexico and Peru.

Leaving Mexico, Cabrillo's ships headed north, hugging the coastline, naming features they encountered, and making observations of the terrain. By September they had reached the expansive and promising bay of San Diego. From there

Cabrillo and his men continued northward, stopping at San Clemente and Santa Catalina Islands. Here the Spanish reported seeing "a great number of Indians who came out of the bushes and grass, shouting, dancing, and making signs to come ashore."[2] Though the Spaniards observed women fleeing as their ships approached, Cabrillo and his men apparently managed to assure the islanders that they did not intend to do harm, gave the Indians gifts, and left the same day.

The next day Cabrillo's ships continued to explore the coastline, stopping in a sheltered bay they named the "Bay of Smokes," perhaps because of smoke rising from Indian fires on the mainland. Some have conjectured that this was Santa Monica Bay, while others think San Pedro Bay a more likely possibility. In either case, when a canoe came out to meet the Spanish ships it most certainly was manned by coastal Gabrielino.

What the Gabrielino thought as they saw Cabrillo's ships sail into view will never be known. However, it is quite possible that they viewed these strangers with apprehension. True, Alta California's coastal people had never seen a Spaniard before, but some had already heard tales from the interior of fearsome, strangely dressed intruders. Cabrillo was informed by the native people he met near San Diego that "men like us were traveling about, bearded, clothed and armed . . . killing many native Indians."[3] When the Gabrielino met Cabrillo near Santa Monica, they used signs to relate a similar story. These reports most likely stemmed from another Spanish expedition, under Francisco Vásquez de Coronado, which had penetrated into the Arizona and New Mexico area shortly before Cabrillo's voyage and had left a very unfavorable impression among the natives there. For the time being, however, the Gabrielino did not have much to fear. The Spanish ships soon departed northward and, by the time they passed Santa Monica again on their return voyage, Cabrillo himself was dead and the expedition was weakened by hunger and scurvy.

The enduring result of Cabrillo's voyage was that, as far as Europe was concerned, all of Alta California now belonged to Spain. However, Spain's claim of ownership had little immediate effect on the native people of the Santa Monica area. Instead, Santa Monica was a place the Spanish passed by on their way to somewhere else. Spain operated a fleet of trading ships—the Manila Galleons—that shuttled between Mexico and the Philippines at least once a year starting in 1565. Their return trip entailed sailing down the California coast past Santa Monica Bay. For about 200 years the Gabrielino observed the regular passing of these ships and these "huge houses on the sea" became legendary among them. Some tantalizing, but unsubstantiated, stories suggest that these galleons, or perhaps the pirate ships that harassed them, sometimes anchored in Santa Monica Bay and sent crews ashore to get fresh water from Santa Monica Canyon. However, there is not much evidence the Gabrielino were affected by these comings and goings. Similarly, a little-documented coastal voyage led by Sebastián Cermeño in 1595 and another Spanish exploratory voyage headed by Sebastián Vizcaíno in 1602 both passed the Santa Monica area. Both retraced much of

Cabrillo's route and Vizcaíno gave many new names to the places he saw, but neither voyage appears to have had much effect on the region or its inhabitants.

Difficult to reach from Spain's base in Mexico, and with no obvious riches to take advantage of, the Santa Monica area, along with the rest of Alta California, was neglected by the Spanish for the next two centuries. Starting in the sixteenth century the Spanish did have a dramatic effect on many North American native groups—in territory ranging from Florida all the way to New Mexico—as Spain expanded and consolidated her New World frontiers. But unlike other areas claimed by Spain, such as Florida, Alta California played only a small strategic role in the battle for New World resources the country was waging with its main competitors England and France. As a result, the Gabrielino were among the last North American peoples to experience the clash of European and native cultures. Indeed, the Gabrielino remained in control of Santa Monica until the Spanish began to turn their full attention to the area much later.

It was in the 1760s, when Spain abandoned its policy of benign neglect for Alta California, that things really began to change. By this time the Spanish began to fear other European powers would find uses for the region and profit from the access it offered to the Pacific. Spain saw immediate threats from Russia and England. Russia posed a problem because fur hunters from Siberia had begun expanding their operations into the Pacific Basin, occupying the Aleutian Islands. Spain feared the Russians might descend into Alta California, establish settlements, and challenge Spain's claim to the region. Meanwhile, Spanish authorities worried that English explorers from Canada or Louisiana might find a waterway across the continent, thereby giving the English easy access to the Pacific. These brewing tensions spurred Gaspar de Portolá's 1769 expedition to Alta California and began the transformation of the region into an active Spanish colony.

Portolá was a seasoned military man who had only been in the New World for a couple of years before he was called upon to secure Alta California for Spain. His task was formidable—not only was Portolá expected to explore terrain that Europeans had never traversed, traveling all the way from Baja California to Monterey, he was also charged with establishing two settlements, one in San Diego and one in Monterey, each with both military and missionary functions. Despite a series of mishaps and near disasters, Portolá succeeded on both counts. Though both settlements were far from the Santa Monica area, they formed the beginnings of active settlement that would soon spawn outposts in other parts of Alta California.

Aside from Portolá's success in staking out a better claim to Alta California, his expedition also observed and recorded much of what they saw as they traveled through what was, to them, an utterly foreign land. Although many members of the expedition were already sick or disabled by the time they arrived in San Diego, Portolá had about sixty healthy men and a long train of mules to carry supplies as he set out towards Monterey. He described the trip to the Los Angeles area as fraught with "the greatest hardships and difficulties" but the group succeeded in reaching the approximate area of today's La Cienega Park, where La Cienega Boulevard and Olympic Boulevard meet, on August 3, 1769. In describing what they saw that day Miguel Costansó, the expedition's cartographer, observed, "All the country we saw on this day's march appeared to us most suitable for the production of all kinds of grain and fruits."[4] This astute observation would certainly be borne out by the great agricultural productivity of the region in the decades and centuries to come.

On August 4, they proceeded from the La Cienega Park area to a place near the present Veterans Administration complex northeast of Santa Monica, about four miles from the coast. The exact location is debated, but many believe it was on the site where University High School now stands. Father Juan Crespí, one of the diarists of the expedition, made these notes of the group's experiences there:

> After two hours' travel, during which we must have covered about two leagues, we stopped at the watering place, which consists of two little springs that rise at the foot of a higher mesa. From each of the two springs runs a small stream of water which is soon absorbed; they are both full of watercress and innumerable bushes of Castillian roses. We made camp near the springs, where we found a good village of very friendly and docile Indians, who, as soon as we arrived, came to visit us, bringing their presents of baskets of sage and other seeds, small, round nuts with a hard shell, and large and very sweet acorns. They made me a present of some strings of beads of white and red shells which resemble coral, though not very fine; we reciprocated with glass beads. I understood that they were asking us if we were going to stay, and I said "No," that we were going farther on. I called this place San Gregorio, but to the soldiers the spot is known as the Springs of El Berrendo, because they caught a deer alive there, it having had a leg broken the preceding afternoon by a shot fired by one of the volunteer soldiers, who could not overtake it. The water is in a hollow surrounded by low hills not far from the sea.[5]

It was this moment—when Portolá and his men were so near to Santa Monica—that inspired a much-repeated legend of how Santa Monica got its name. The story goes that after having said mass with another priest, Father Crespí named the place *Las Lagrimas de Santa Monica* because the pure water of the spring reminded him of the tears of Saint Monica—the fourth-century mother of Saint Augustine. (Apparently Saint Augustine, before becoming a pious Christian and major theologian, did much to provoke his mother to tears.) Some versions of this legend have even placed Father Junipero Serra at the scene when this naming occurred. While this is a colorful addition, it is inaccurate. Though Serra was part of the expedition to found San Diego and Monterey in 1769, he went by ship rather than on foot and therefore wasn't anywhere near Santa Monica at the time. Similarly, there is no reason to think that Father Crespí named the place he saw on August 4 anything other than what he wrote in his diary—San Gregorio—a name that obviously did not stick. Indeed, the true origin of the name Santa Monica is shrouded in mystery. We know only that by the 1820s the name was already in use—the first official mention being an 1827 grazing permit for "the place called Santa Monica."

In any case, the explorers had more on their minds than names. They also had to find a route by which they could proceed on to Monterey. From San Gregorio the explorers hoped to regain the coast and continue northward, but when Portolá sent scouts ahead to check the route he was disappointed with the news. Costansó wrote:

> The scouts who had been sent out to examine the coast and the road along the beach returned shortly afterwards with the news of having reached a steep, high cliff, terminating in the sea where the mountains end, absolutely cutting off passage along the shore.[6]

Though opinions differ, it is likely that the scouts had reached the northwest end of today's Palisades Park and seen Santa Monica Canyon as the obstacle to their progress along the coast. As a result, the expedition headed off through the San Fernando Valley and was not seen again so near to Santa Monica.

Having seen Spaniards in the flesh the native people of the region may have wondered what their purpose was here. In asking Crespí whether the expedition intended to stay in the area, the Gabrielino were not asking an idle question, but one they knew had serious implications. Indeed, accounts of the Gabrielino reaction to the Spanish indicate that they viewed these interlopers with suspicion and unease, despite their outward signs of hospitality. In describing the Gabrielinos' early meetings with the Spanish, Hugo Reid, a nineteenth-century authority on Los Angeles's Indians who had access to native informants, reported:

> The Indians were sadly afraid when they saw the Spaniards coming on horseback. Thinking them gods, the women ran to the brush and hid themselves, while the men put out fires in their huts. . . . An occurrence however soon convinced them that their strange visitors were, like themselves, mortals, for one of the Spaniards leveled his musket at a bird and killed it. Although greatly terrified at the report of the piece, yet the effect it produced of taking life, led them to reason, and deduce the impossibility of the "Giver of Life" to murder animals. . . . They consequently put them down as human beings of a nasty white color, and having ugly blue eyes![7]

Apparently the Indians were also less pleased with the gifts the Spaniards gave them than they let on. While the Gabrielino graciously accepted all the food they were offered by the Spanish, they were repulsed by the foreign food and buried it secretly in the woods. In this context, the Gabrielino may have been relieved that, for the moment, the Spanish did not intend to stay. Instead, Portolá's goal was reaching Monterey and the Santa Monica area was only uncivilized land to be crossed in pursuit of solidifying claims elsewhere. Soon enough, however, the growing Spanish presence in Alta California would amount to more than an occasional parley between the native people and a poorly equipped band of explorers.

Realizing that a couple of flimsy settlements in San Diego and Monterey would not suffice to hold Alta California for the Spanish, Spain embarked on the next phase of its plan—the establishment of a series of missions and military outposts (known as *presidios*) running the length of the territory. This strategy of employing missions and military posts as a means of securing Alta California was based on the peculiar remoteness of the region. A land route to Alta California from the main part of Mexico had not yet been mapped. Access by sea from Spain's base of operations in Mexico was difficult because prevailing currents pushed ships southward, not north. This remoteness, as well as the lack of opportunities to get rich quickly, meant few Spanish settlers could be persuaded to come to Alta California. Therefore, Spain sent a limited number of soldiers to man small military bases and relied heavily on missions to "civilize" the rest of Alta California.

Missions had long been used by the Spanish in many parts of North America as part of a policy of bringing Catholicism and Spanish civilization to native peoples. However, by the 1770s missions had lost favor as a means of settlement because they frequently failed to win over the native populations or effectively secure regions where they were implanted. Moreover, the age of religious fervor, which had made conversion of the natives a top priority, had long since given way to a more pragmatic approach in Spain's New World empire.

Ironically, it was this very pragmatism that made missions seem useful for Alta California. By bringing native peoples into missions and Hispanicizing them, the meager number of Spanish settlers could be offset. Not only that, under the mission system the Indians themselves did almost all the work of bringing virgin lands under cultivation, constructing buildings, building roads, and the like. As a result, the missions had the appeal of being cost effective at a time when Spain's resources in the area were thin. This is not to say that the missionaries themselves viewed their work cynically. On the contrary, the Franciscan fathers saw nothing incompatible in the twin goals of Christianizing Indians while turning them into productive subjects of the Spanish king.

Having decided on this course of action, the Spanish soon established missions throughout Alta California. For the coastal inhabitants of the Santa Monica area, the founding of Mission San Gabriel in 1771 was of greatest importance. Although some Gabrielino persisted in their age-old ways even after the establishment of San Gabriel, none could escape the sweeping effects of Spanish presence in the area.

Although there were tensions initially between the Gabrielino and the Spanish sent to start the mission, the padres succeeded in inducing the Gabrielino to construct the first mission buildings and to baptize some natives. By 1772, the padres had recorded twenty-eight baptisms at the mission, though there is not much evidence that these "neophytes" had altered their customary religious beliefs. (Early on the neophytes understood little or no Spanish and the padres giving religious instruction were equally impaired in Indian languages.) Over time the missionaries claimed more and more converts. Ten years after the mission was founded, the fathers noted that 776 Indians had been baptized and by the end of Spanish rule almost 7,000 Indians had undergone this Christian rite.

The mission fathers' plans were not limited to religious instruction alone. Indeed, with baptism came an entirely new life—one that could not have been more different from the way the Gabrielino had been accustomed to live. Once attached to a mission, an Indian stood as a child in relation to the mission fathers. Every aspect of his or her day was regulated and constrained with strict hours for waking, work, worship, eating, and sleeping. Since the Indians themselves were relied on to clear the land, plant, harvest, mill, make wine, weave, and perform a whole host of other industrious activities, work responsibilities weighed heavily on men and women alike. Not surprisingly, many Indians resisted this regimented life and it is estimated that at any given moment one out of every ten mission Indians was actively planning an escape. However, missionized Indians were never free to come and go at will and escapees were often pursued, captured, and harshly punished.

Yet the pull of the mission on Indian life was very difficult to oppose. Those in the immediate vicinity of Mission San Gabriel saw their lands encroached upon by newly cultivated fields and their gathering grounds trampled and grazed by the livestock the Spanish introduced. As their lands shrank and became less productive, local Indians fled or turned to the mission for sustenance. For those Gabrielino farther afield, pressure to join the mission came more slowly but it came nonetheless. With the agricultural and manufacturing operations at the mission expanding over time, soldiers were sent to Gabrielino villages in the outlying areas to round up new recruits. Brought together without regard to village, linguistic, or tribal affinity and prohibited from practicing many of their customary ways, missionized Indians gradually lost the ability to sustain their native ways. Since Indians who had been converted "lost caste," their relations with non-Mission Indians were fractured and social relations were transformed. And each new generation born at the mission was one more step removed from the Gabrielino culture that had once flourished in Southern California.

Exactly when the Indians of the Santa Monica area came under the direct sway of Mission San Gabriel is unclear. In the 1780s the Spanish governor of Alta California, Pedro Fages, stated that the extreme limit from which converts could effectively be drawn was less than twenty miles away. Present-day Santa Monica lying approximately twenty miles from the mission was, therefore, just beyond the mission's direct grasp. However, even remote Gabrielino villages were affected by affairs in San Gabriel. For one, the presence of San Gabriel disrupted trading networks and interfered with the normal flow of goods to and from the coast. Moreover, though the native inhabitants of the Santa Monica area may have avoided living at the mission, coastal and island Indians sometimes made the trip inland to attend fiestas organized by the neophytes and encouraged by the padres as a way of attracting new converts. This exposure, as well as contact with European novelties such as coins, metal tools, and other items, meant that even Gabrielino people at some distance from the mission felt what one historian has called the "transformative power of European culture."[8]

In addition, the environmental changes caused by Spanish introduction of non-native animals and plants were profound. Ecosystems change constantly but the ecological effects that occurred when the Spanish moved into North American frontier areas like Alta California were dramatic and long-lasting. In fact, ecological change was so swift and irrepressible that several European-introduced plants arrived in remote Alta California even before actual Europeans did, their seeds having been inadvertently carried overland by Indian travelers or animals, or dispersed by natural forces from places the Spanish had already visited like New Mexico. As new plants were changing the landscape and altering the natural environment the Gabrielino were accustomed to, the animals introduced by the Spanish in the 1770s were making themselves at home as well. Both cattle and horses found the grazing and climate of the Southern California coast ideal, and herds quickly grew and spread across the area. By 1813, for example, the mission at San Gabriel possessed 13,000 head of cattle and 11,000 sheep. When they gathered together at watering places these animals crushed native plants and compacted the soil. When heavy rains fell, water then rushed through, creating the arroyos that are now a well-known feature of the Los Angeles area landscape. As water sped away over the hard ground, rather than seeping into the soil, once-lush grasslands that had supported a host of animals and birds were degraded. These unintended consequences of Spanish settlement affected the Gabrielinos' ability to sustain their traditional ways as surely as the more active efforts of the missionaries. Over time, even the natural environment of areas at some distance from the mission, such as Santa Monica, would be transformed permanently.

Most devastating of all for the Gabrielino, however, were the effects of the killing diseases inadvertently introduced by the Spanish. The Gabrielino had no natural resistance to many of the germs Europeans carried and they died in staggering numbers. Measles and influenza killed many. Tuberculosis, dysentery, and smallpox, which spread easily in the crowded and unsanitary living quarters at the missions, felled more. And venereal disease, which may have been spread early on by members of Portolá's expedition but was certainly carried by the Spanish soldiers living near the mission, weakened many Gabrielino adults and infected children born to them. As a result, by the 1810s the mission fathers were obliged to report that "the number of deaths is double that of births" among the missionized Indians.[9] Mortality in villages near Santa Monica was probably no better as these same diseases spread rapidly and easily to all the Gabrielino settlements in the area. For this reason alone, the coming of the Spanish was a dire calamity for the Gabrielino, whether they were in San Gabriel or Santa Monica. This demographic disaster reduced the number of able-bodied adults who could hunt and gather, tore families and villages apart, undermined traditional spiritual and cultural practices, increased the Gabrielinos' dependence on the mission, and made real resistance to the Spanish virtually impossible.

Despite these horrific results, the mission was a success from the Spanish point of view. The missionaries' intent had been to convert the natives to Christianity and bring the land under cultivation and there is no disputing that these objectives were reached, even if the cost to the Gabrielino was exceedingly high. The friars at San Gabriel baptized thousands of Indians and the mission was the most productive of all those established in Alta California. San Gabriel furnished supplies to other less-successful missions and outfitted various expeditions around Alta California. Governor Fages acknowledged Mission San Gabriel's particular importance in 1787: "It is to a great extent true," he said, "that it has sustained the conquest [of California]."[10]

However, San Gabriel's very success helped bring about its downfall. Because the missions were granted control of most of the fertile lands not only around the mission but for miles in all directions, and because the mission largely dominated the available labor force in the region, the mission inspired jealousy among the small secular population at the nearby pueblo of Los Angeles. The pueblo of Los Angeles, founded as a farming community on the Los Angeles River in 1781, was part of Spain's continuing efforts to populate the area with loyal subjects. Its first settlers were a diverse group of forty-four drawn from Mexican villages in Sonora and Sinaloa, accompanied by an escort of soldiers. As such they represented the different racial groups prevalent in Mexico—with Indians, blacks, and individuals of mixed race forming the majority of the group. Though the initial party was small the pueblo took hold, and by the end of the 1780s there were twenty-eight families in the pueblo for a total population of 139.

From the beginning the life of the pueblo was tied to that of San Gabriel. Residents of the town were expected to travel the approximately eight miles to the mission to hear mass, and padres from the mission made the trip to the pueblo to perform various religious services. However, there was tension over a variety of issues. The mission padres suspected the townspeople of corrupting the Indians. The townspeople at times resented having to travel so far for religious services and complained that the padres neglected their needs. And with the mission in control of so much land and labor, eventually the inhabitants of Los Angeles grew to resent the hold the mission had over the area and its economic resources. In fact this resentment was not limited to the Los Angeles pueblo. In other areas of Alta

California as well, the growing population of secular settlers and their civil leaders increasingly chafed at the privileged position of the missions. Thus, when Mexico declared its independence from Spain in 1821, the seeds for the destruction of the mission system had already been sown.

Before long the missions would be history, but the effects of Spanish rule would live on, even in places like Santa Monica that had been inconsequential under Spanish rule. Due to Spain, the region was first mapped and explored by Europeans. Due to Spain, newcomers settled and introduced an entirely different way of life to the area than had been known before. The descendants of these Spanish colonists, the *Californios*, would soon find their way to Santa Monica and make it their own. Due to Spain, the long-time inhabitants of the Santa Monica area—the Gabrielino—were reduced in number, dispersed, and saw their control over the region and their own destiny taken from them. The reduced population of the Santa Monica area left it open to new claimants and made it appear as if the land were a blank slate, on which ambitious immigrants could write their own stories. And due to Spain, the vast agricultural potential of the Los Angeles region was revealed. In sowing wheat, barley, corn, and lentils, in planting grapevines, and in tending sheep and cattle, the missionaries and their native workforce showed just how profitable this part of California could be. And, last but not least, it was due to Spain that the pueblo of Los Angeles was started. From its modest origins this place would grow to have a tremendous influence on the surrounding area, helping to shape, for good or bad, the future city of Santa Monica.

Chapter Three

MEXICAN RANCHOS AND THE COMING

OF THE AMERICANS

By the turn of the nineteenth century, Spain was in crisis due to a series of European wars that had crippled its economy and severed its once-lucrative colonial trade routes. Distracted by the political and economic chaos at home, many of Spain's New World colonies were left to twist in the wind. Moreover, a new political spirit was in the air. Both the American Revolution in 1776 and the French Revolution of the 1790s stirred appetites for freedom from monarchy and colonial rule elsewhere. Spain's colonies in the New World, emboldened by these new political ideas, took advantage of the power vacuum left by Spain's crisis to assert their independence. When Mexico broke free from Spanish rule in 1821, Alta California (increasingly known simply as California) was soon swept along, becoming a territory of Mexico by 1822. Under Mexican rule Santa Monica began to take shape as a place for ranching, under the supervision of the Californios—who were mostly native-born descendants of earlier Spanish settlers. It wasn't long however before this new equilibrium was threatened and yet another new power, this time the United States, would begin to remake the region all over again.

By the time the Spanish flag was exchanged for a Mexican one in 1822, California was home to a chain of well-established missions (some, like San Gabriel, were extensive and very productive operations), some military outposts known as presidios, and a few growing towns. It was still, however, a remote region with few connections to the outside world. And despite Spain's more than two and a half centuries of rule, California's Native American population of 100,000 or more still vastly exceeded the estimated 3,200 Hispanics in the region.

It was also a place of simmering tensions among these Hispanic residents. The Franciscan fathers who ran the missions had long been accustomed to dominating all the best land along the coast from San Francisco to San Diego, as had been their right under Spanish rule. In their efforts to "civilize" the Indians, the mission fathers were also used to monopolizing unpaid Indian labor. This did not always sit well with settlers eager to improve their fortunes in California. In pueblos like Los Angeles, which had reached a population of 850 by the end of the colonial period, residents resented the advantages Mission San Gabriel enjoyed, and with good reason. As historian David Weber has remarked, "missions and presidios both stood as obstacles to economic opportunity for would-be colonists in a dangerous and distant land." Even worse, the mission fathers "worked assiduously to stifle the growth of civil towns and of private ranches."[11] When Mexican rule came, it did not help that some Franciscans refused to swear allegiance to the new government.

Under these circumstances, it is not surprising that the missions were dismantled and their land and property dispersed during the Mexican period. Although official Mexican policy varied over time, its end result was that, by 1834, the missions were "secularized," new mission administrators were appointed by the Mexican government, and mission land, animals, and equipment speedily found their way into private hands. Under Spain, mission land and property had been held by the fathers "in trust" for their Indian charges. It had always been understood that the Indians were the de facto owners of the land and that their work, in theory at least, was for their own benefit. Now, despite a policy that ostensibly gave Indians one-half of mission lands, livestock, and farm tools, mission property was appropriated not only by local Hispanics but also by the government, which considered mission property a form of revenue. At San Gabriel, the Indians held secret meetings, met with the mission's new administrators, and attempted to regain some of their rights but to no avail. Over a relatively short period of time, Mission San Gabriel was stripped of most of its valuable property and the Indians there were forced to find new ways to support themselves.

This process was formalized in the land grants that were issued to private individuals in the hundreds under the Mexican regime. In California as a whole, only about thirty land grants had been dispensed during the Spanish period, and those were not grants of ownership but rather concessions allowing use of a given property for a limited time. The Spanish government always retained rights of ownership. The Mexican government, in contrast, used outright gifts of land as a way of encouraging settlers to populate California, the only requirements being that grantees be Mexican citizens (either native-born or naturalized) and Catholic. From 1822 until 1846 hundreds of large land grants were handed out by the Mexican government, many of which were carved out of former mission properties that the Indians had painstakingly improved. In this process, the Los Angeles Basin, including the Santa Monica area, was divvied up into ranchos that extended from the mountains all the way to the sea. (The former Indian inhabitants of the missions, meanwhile, were occasionally given small plots of land for their own, but had great difficulty in securing legal title even to these allotments.) So, after decades of constraints under the thumb of Spain, it was now the Californios turn to enjoy exceptional advantages. As Alfred Robinson, who lived in California at the time, observed, "Many [Spanish and Mexican-Californians] that were poor soon became wealthy, the possessors of farms, which they stocked with cattle."[12]

The Mexican era brought private ownership of the land to Santa Monica for the first time. Under Spanish rule nearby parcels of land had been allotted to private individuals for grazing use. For example, in 1804 Rancho Topanga Malibu Sequit, extending for miles up the coast near Santa Monica, was given to one José Bartolomé Tapia. Although Santa Monica itself may have been used as grazing land for cattle from this and other nearby concessions, and the Gabrielino may have continued to use it as part of their traditional territory, it was not until 1828 that some of this land became private property.

Santa Monica

The history of the Santa Monica ranchos has been fraught with confusion, in part because of lengthy legal disputes that clouded the claims of different rancheros. However, the first claim to Santa Monica lands seems to have been given jointly to Francisco Javier Alvarado and Antonio Ignacio Machado as a grazing permit, allowing the two men to use the coastal land from Santa Monica Canyon to Topanga Canyon, as well as some inland acreage. Machado's interest in the area did not last long however, and by 1831 he had turned over his rights to Alvarado, who died soon afterwards. The right to use the land for grazing remained in the hands of Alvarado's sons until 1838 when they, in turn, relinquished the privilege to two residents of Los Angeles—a blacksmith named Francisco Marquez and a landowner and grape-grower named Ysidro Reyes.

Exactly what brought these two men together is not known. No doubt their paths crossed in Los Angeles, which was still small enough for everyone to know everyone else. Marquez was already forty years old and represented the immigrant element in the growing pueblo of Los Angeles. Born in Guadalajara, Mexico, in 1798, Marquez had immigrated to Los Angeles in 1825 where he set up a blacksmith and harness shop, trades that must have been much in demand in horse-dependent Los Angeles. Meanwhile Reyes, only twenty-seven years old, was a native Californio, born in Los Angeles in 1811. Around the time of his land grant application, Reyes was a married man living in an adobe on Fourth and Main Streets in the pueblo.

In 1838, soon after obtaining the old grazing permit, these two men applied for formal ownership of the place called Santa Monica, making the proper petition to the governor in Monterey as well as submitting a map of their proposed rancho. Rancho Boca de Santa Monica, so named because it included the mouth of Santa Monica Canyon, was to extend over 6,657 acres stretching from Topanga Canyon southeastward to where present-day Montana Avenue reaches the palisades. From the beach it extended inland to today's Fernwood above Topanga Canyon and to Sullivan Canyon in the east. Marquez in particular may have felt confident in his claim, as he was already a fixture in Santa Monica Canyon well before 1838. Indeed, he had set up a blacksmith's workshop there as early as 1831. For the moment, things did go smoothly. Their grant was approved by the governor and the relevant local officials traveled from Los Angeles to survey the land and execute the necessary formalities. Thus, by 1839 Marquez and Reyes were able to officially take title to the land. But though they were to remain in possession of the property well past the Mexican period, they were almost immediately embroiled in a legal dispute with another claimant.

Unfortunately, the Rancho Boca de Santa Monica boundaries came into direct conflict with those of a rancho already granted in 1828, to Francisco Sepúlveda. Originally named Rancho San Vicente, and later renamed Rancho San Vicente y Santa Monica after the dispute was underway, Sepúlveda's property extended over the same territory from Santa Monica Canyon to Topanga Canyon, but it reached a great deal further inland. Starting in 1839 and dragging on for decades, the competing claims were repeatedly surveyed, the courts attempted to sort out the mess, and Los Angeles society took sides, each supporting their favorite claim. The end result—decided in the 1880s after the original rancheros were long dead—was that the 1839 Rancho Boca de Santa Monica claim to 6,657 acres was verified while 30,260 acres inland were confirmed for Rancho San Vicente y Santa Monica.

Another rancho in the Santa Monica area created less contention. Rancho La Ballona (also known as Rancho Paso de las Carretas) was formally granted in 1839 to brothers José Augustin and Ignacio Machado, and to brothers Felipe and Tomás Talamantes. (The Machado family seems to have occupied and had rights to some of this ranch even under Spanish rule.) Comprising 13,920 acres in all, this rancho was located south of Rancho Boca de Santa Monica and extended over territory that would later become the Ocean Park district of the city of Santa Monica, Venice, Palms, Marina del Rey, Playa del Rey, Mar Vista, and a large part of Culver City.

As a result of these land grants from the Mexican government, a small number of families—the Machados and Talamantes at La Ballona, the Reyes and Marquez clans at Boca de Santa Monica, and the Sepúlvedas of San Vicente y Santa Monica—became the barons of the Santa Monica area. Throughout the Mexican period and persisting even after California became part of the United States, these ranching families stood at the apex of an almost feudal system that allowed a great deal of ease and enjoyment for the Californios themselves, while relying on Indians for almost all of the labor required to make these lands profitable. Supporting the whole rancho system was one commodity—cattle.

Mission San Gabriel pioneered many innovations in the Los Angeles Basin, successfully planting many new crops and fostering industries such as candle and textile production. However, it was cattle, not crops or crafts, that the Californios of the Mexican period found most interesting. Cattle formed the backbone of the rancho economy partly because, with secularization of the missions, they were easily available. Indeed, the thousands of cattle that were formerly mission property were often "borrowed" to start new herds on the ranchos. (In 1834, Mission San Gabriel possessed 16,500 head of cattle but by 1840 only 100 remained.) Moreover, unlike agriculture that required the land to be cleared, tilled, and intensively tended before it could be profitable, cattle could be raised on unimproved and unfenced land and pretty much took care of themselves until they were needed for meat, hides, or tallow.

In the years before the Gold Rush, cattle provided a livelihood for Santa Monica's ranching families because hides were a valuable raw material on the international market. Ships from Spain, the United States, and other countries called at depots along the California coast, including San Pedro, to collect the thousands of hides the ranchos produced each year. From there the hides were transported to places like New England, where they were made into shoes and other leather articles. Tallow—rendered animal fat—was also collected in large vats and taken aboard ships to be made into candles in distant lands. As the most valuable parts of the animal at the time, hides commanded about $2 each and the tallow from each animal was worth another $2, affording the ranchers a comfortable income.

Santa Monica

The hide and tallow trade wove Santa Monica's ranchos along with the rest of California into an international trading network for the first time. In fact, the California ranchos in the 1830s and 1840s were totally dependent on this trade for their prosperity. The ranchers neither built ships of their own to transport their raw materials to market, nor did they manufacture most of the finished goods required for daily life such as shoes, clothing, or furniture. Thus when ships came to collect hides and tallow, they also brought with them desirable items made elsewhere. Richard Henry Dana, who wrote an account of his experiences working in the California hide trade in *Two Years before the Mast*, listed some of the goods ranchers acquired from the merchant ships:

> . . . teas, coffee, sugars, spices, raisins, molasses, spirits of all kinds (sold by the cask), hardware, crockery, tinware, cutlery, clothing of all kinds, boots and shoes, calico and cotton cloth, silks, shawls, scarfs, necklaces and other jewelry, combs, furniture . . . and in fact, everything that can be imagined, from Chinese fireworks to English cart wheels.[13]

This trade was not limited to the legitimate ships that duly paid taxes to the Mexican government. Smugglers were an accepted part of life and Santa Monica's beaches were among the locations smugglers used in transferring their clandestine cargoes. This trade, both legal and not, along with the overland pack trains that started arriving from Santa Fe in the 1830s, raised the standard of living for the Californios living on ranchos in the Los Angeles Basin.

With their large tracts of land, their vast herds of cattle, and an increasingly genteel existence, the ranchers did quite well into the 1840s. The Gold Rush made them richer still. After 1849, when news of the discovery of gold in Northern California spread around the world, thousands of newcomers swarmed to California and they were hungry. Beef, which had been virtually worthless before the Gold Rush (compared to the value of hides and tallow), was now in great demand. Southern California's ranchers quickly grasped that money could be made by driving their cattle up north where steers might sell for $50 to $70 or more a head. By the 1850s the price of cattle was sky high and cash was pouring into the hands of the old Californio ranching families.

Under such favorable circumstances, Hispanic ranching families flourished. Although Santa Monica was still a wild place where bears and other native animals roamed freely, the early families built homes and succeeded in making the land their own. Francisco Marquez built the first adobe on Rancho Boca de Santa Monica lands, in Santa Monica Canyon where San Lorenzo Street is today. Meanwhile, Ysidro Reyes constructed his first ranch house west of Rustic Canyon in today's Pacific Palisades. In 1834 Reyes constructed a second residence near today's Seventh Street and Adelaide Drive. The oldest structure from this era that still survives in Santa Monica is a house built in the

1840s at 404 Georgina Avenue. The original adobe section of this house was used by ranch hands from Sepulveda's Rancho San Vicente y Santa Monica. With the ranchers growing wealthy their houses grew larger, better furnished, and more comfortable.

Much has been written about the idyllic way of life on Californio ranchos in this period. Santa Monica was both sparsely settled and remote, but that did not prevent the Californios from creating their own diversions such as fiestas organized around important events like weddings, the roundup of cattle, or religious holidays. Gatherings were also an excuse for horse races and other shows of masculine skill. Generous hospitality was a hallmark of rancho culture. Visiting Californios or foreigners were welcomed warmly and it was said that a man could travel the whole length of California without a horse or resources of his own, simply borrowing horses from ranches along the way and depending on the kindness of the ranchers for hearty meals and agreeable lodging.

As they grew richer with the Gold Rush, Californio ranchers could afford to be generous not only with visitors but with themselves, and Los Angeles provided many opportunities to spend money. Most Los Angeles area ranchers maintained residences in the pueblo of Los Angeles—the true center of social and economic life for the region—as well as homes on their ranchos. Santa Monica's ranchers were no exception. Ysidro Reyes always kept a townhouse in Los Angeles as his primary residence and Francisco Sepúlveda lived there as well, not far from the plaza. Just as the adobes on the ranchos were made more comfortable over time, the rancheros spent money to expand their townhouses and fill them with items such as lace-curtained four-poster beds imported from abroad. Never likely to neglect their personal appearance, ranchers and their families also spent lavishly on clothing. One member of the Sepúlveda clan spent the phenomenal sum of $1,000 for his suits and outfitted his horses equally richly. Gambling was also a much appreciated pastime for ranchers in Los Angeles and it too absorbed some of the cash that poured into the hands of these fortunate Californios.

With productive and profitable estates, luxuries to enjoy, and a lively social life under sunny skies, life in the early and mid-nineteenth century was certainly good for Santa Monica's ranching families. No wonder their lifestyle has been so romanticized by subsequent generations of Southern Californians. But the rancho system was a hierarchical system and the Californio ranchers—in Santa Monica and elsewhere—were but the top layer. Underneath them, performing almost all the labor on the ranchos, was a large Native American workforce that existed in abject peonage. When the missions were disbanded and their property dispersed among the Hispanic residents of the area, the mission Indians were left to patch together what livelihood they could. Some fled into the mountain and desert areas of California where the land was not yet encroached on by ranchos. Many others saw little choice but to remain on the land and work for the new masters who claimed it. The ranchers were, for their part, more than happy for the Indians to remain since land alone was of little value without the labor to work it. Many former mission Indians also possessed essential skills that were as useful on the ranches as they had been at the missions. Thus the population living on an average Southern California rancho consisted of the owner and his large family (including perhaps some poor relations) and a much larger number of Indians who did everything from domestic chores, such as cooking and cleaning, to the work of herding and slaughtering cattle, to preparing hides and rendering tallow. Indians also drove the *carretas* that transported both people and goods at the time, guarded their master's property, and took care of the numerous other tasks a working ranch required.

Meanwhile, contemporary observers reported, the Californios performed only work that could be done on horseback, a pattern that seems to have been ingrained from the earliest days of the Los Angeles pueblo. A 1796 report on Los Angeles by two Catholic priests was already noting the tendency of settlers to employ Indians to do "nearly everything" in terms of labor.[14] Throughout the Mexican period and into the time when California became a state, not much changed in that respect. Indeed, as Benjamin Wilson reported in his assessment of Southern California's Indians in 1852, "Indians built all the houses in the country, and planted all the fields and vineyards." They "mix with us hourly. . . . They are almost the only house or farm servants we have."[15]

But essential though they were to the success of Southern California's ranchos, Indians were seen as a class apart and generally treated poorly. They earned less for their work than others might, often only enough for their basic food, clothing, and shelter. Without resources of their own or legal protection, they were not free to move about in search of better employment, and they had little recourse if they were cheated or denied their due. In the worst cases reported for Los Angeles in the mid-nineteenth century, Indians were paid partially in liquor and then, when they became inebriated, were arrested for drunkenness. As punishment they were bound out to labor again and were again paid partially in alcohol, only to begin the vicious cycle again. Certainly not all Indians received such abominable treatment—the lives of native workers on ranches no doubt differed quite a bit in quality—but Indians never enjoyed the same level of privilege as their Californio, and later American, masters.

Unfortunately, only a few stories of the Indians who lived on Santa Monica's ranchos survive. Herminia Reyes, granddaughter of one of the original grantees of Rancho Boca de Santa Monica, recalled that in the early years of the rancho "the nearest neighbors of the Reyes and Marquez families were Indians" who lived, at least part of the year, in native villages at Santa Ynez, Malibu, Topanga Canyon, and Playa del Rey. Rancho Boca de Santa Monica also had resident Indians and Herminia recalled how:

> Every morning, rain or shine, the head of the family would get up at dawn, to sing the "Alva" a religious song, then the rosary would be recited. All the family had to get up, kneel and pray. The Indians and other servants would kneel out in the patios. Then they would be ready to start the day.[16]

This recollection, brief though it is, clearly evokes the way in which the Indians' and their employers' lives were at once intertwined but separate. Another story told by Herminia Reyes is worth quoting in full:

> My ancestors had carratas [*sic*] with ox-teams to travel to Los Angeles [from Santa Monica]. They had no direct roads. In dry weather they made what they called a cut-off across the Cienega and what is now Culver City, to what are now Washington and Adams Boulevards.
>
> Indians would walk ahead with a gauacha or long pole to try to scare up the cattle that would happen to be lying in the way. In wet weather they traveled to Westwood, Sherman and Hollywood. It would sometimes take three or four days to get to Los Angeles. The carratas had large wooden wheels cut from large trees, usually sycamore, of which there were plenty on our own ranchos. Four poles, one at each corner, a canopy was stretched over if the family was traveling.
>
> Hanging on the poles, they always had a cangelon, or horn with soap preparation, which they always put on the wheels at intervals, so the wheels would not burn. When out of soap they would cut cactus and put it in the wheels.
>
> Once in a pinch when there was no cactus, grandmother ordered the Indians to put in some rice pudding which they happened to have for their lunch. The Indian would throw a spoonful of pudding in the wheel and one in his mouth and say, it is a shame to feed the pudding to a wheel.[17]

This story tells of many interesting things—the long distances to travel, the primitive mode of transportation, the fact that cattle were everywhere—but it also gives an example of one of the many duties Indians performed, how such servants were accustomed to walk for days while their superiors rode, and the fact that an Indian might give up his lunch if ordered to, but not without feeling the loss of it.

Whether one was at the bottom or the top of the rancho hierarchy, it wasn't long before the whole system was disrupted. Indeed, Mexican rule of California was destined to last only twenty-six years. Once California became American in 1848, the rancho way of life slowly began to unravel. Before too long, Santa Monica's time as an unfenced pasture dotted with the occasional adobe would end. And just as Santa Monica's native people had once been displaced, the Californios too would soon find themselves elbowed aside, their dominance of the region slipping away.

Americans were on the move west in the nineteenth century and from 1826, when Jedediah Smith became the first to arrive overland from the east, the Los Angeles area increasingly felt their presence. During the period of Mexican rule, the Americans who trickled in had often married into Californio families and adopted the rancho lifestyle as their own.

However, in 1845 the United States government went to war with Mexico over Texas and Mexico was defeated. The result was the 1848 Treaty of Guadalupe Hidalgo in which Mexico ceded nearly all the territory now included in Arizona, western Colorado, Nevada, Utah, Texas, California, and New Mexico to the United States. By 1850, California had become the thirty-first state in the Union. Santa Monica had once again changed hands.

Although Santa Monica's ranchos continued to operate much as before even after American rule began, changes were underway. Because of the Gold Rush, Americans, along with large numbers of fortune seekers from other countries, descended on California. In the process Los Angeles became increasingly multi-ethnic. From its first days Hispanic and black residents had been part of the pueblo of Los Angeles. Now, in addition to incoming Americans, many Mexicans, particularly from Sonora, passed through Los Angeles on their way to the goldfields of Northern California. Chinese men, fleeing poverty and strife in their homeland, appeared in the 1850s and began to build a significant Chinatown. Added to this were handfuls of people from many other nations.

Besides raising the price of beef and swelling the pueblo's population, some of these newcomers—American or otherwise—added a lawless element to the pueblo. Indeed, by the mid-1850s Los Angeles had been transformed into a center for gambling, prostitution, drunkenness, and crime in which brazen murders were a daily occurrence.

Santa Monica's ranching families, with so many ties to Los Angeles, certainly felt their quality of life change in the pueblo as these newcomers imposed their anarchic ways. Meanwhile, the Indians in the area felt the brunt of increased violence and mistreatment as Americans, accustomed to despise Indians, added to their woes. The result for Santa Monica itself, however, was that it became a tourist destination for the first time. Through the feverish years of the Gold Rush the pueblo of Los Angeles grew—jumping from a population of 1,250 in 1845 to 4,385 by 1860. Outside the boundaries of the town, the number of people scattered across the Los Angeles Basin also grew. These Angelinos, as well as travelers from more distant points, wanted a place to escape to and they found it in Santa Monica.

Tourists were particularly attracted to Santa Monica Canyon, which offered shady sycamore glades, fresh water, access to the beach, and pleasant camping and picnicking areas. (The rest of the Santa Monica area continued to be given over to cattle and sheep rather than tourists until significantly later.) Tradition has it that the first user of the canyon as a leisure spot was one "Dr. Hayward," who, along with his family, enjoyed summer camping there as early as 1855. But travelers certainly visited before this. Indeed, the fascinating story of Biddy Mason—a black woman who would go on to be an important member of Los Angeles's African-American community—illustrates how the larger world was already making itself felt in out-of-the-way Santa Monica.

Biddy Mason first came to California in a move from Mississippi in 1851 as a slave accompanying her master, Robert Smith. By 1854 Smith decided to move to Texas, a slave state, and intended to take his slaves with him. On their way there, he, his family, and their slaves stopped for a few days at "a canyon near Santa Monica." But his visit was probably not as relaxing as he had hoped. As Mason's daughter explained:

> they had spent only a few days [in the canyon] when news reached Los Angeles, through a Mrs. Rowen, of San Bernardino, that these slaves were leaving California to go back into slavery in Texas. The sheriff of Los Angeles County, who, at that date (January 19, 1854), was a Mr. Frank Dewitt, issued a writ against this slave-master, preventing him from taking his slaves from the State of California.[18]

Thanks to this intervention, Biddy Mason was subsequently freed, left the canyon, and went on to her illustrious career as a pioneering member of Los Angeles's black community. Even as early as 1854, Santa Monica was not beyond the reach of the controversy over slavery that was engulfing the rest of the United States in the decade before the Civil War.

By the 1860s the reputation of Santa Monica Canyon had grown and was attracting many regular visitors. For example, on September 22, 1867, a San Bernardino newspaper reported the following:

> Picnic.—On Sunday last, almost the entire Hebrew portion of our community went to Santa Monica on a picnic excursion. Three of Banning's six-horse coaches and one of Tomlinson's and Co's [*sic*] conveyed the excursionists to the scene of festivity, where the day was spent in the most delightful manner.[19]

Increasingly, people from Los Angeles made the trip to the coast to sing around campfires, dance, or pursue the rumor circulating at the time that gold might be found in a rock that was only visible at low tide. So agreeable was the setting that some families spent entire summers camping near the mouth of the canyon. Meanwhile, the Californio owners and residents of Rancho Boca de Santa Monica, within whose boundaries the canyon fell, were tolerant of these pleasure-seekers but carried on their ranching activities much as before. Without a doubt though, the ambiance of "old" Santa Monica was changing.

Indeed, by the 1870s the canyon had developed into a full-blown resort with facilities to accommodate hundreds of guests. In 1871 B.L. Peel built a large tent that could sleep up to thirty families. In 1872 a proper hotel was opened for those who preferred more privacy. And eventually the canyon featured, in addition to hotels, a small grocery store, a bathhouse, butcher shop, dancehall, and drinking establishments. Camping remained very popular into the 1870s as well. An Iowan visiting Santa Monica in 1877 recorded her impressions of:

a narrow, little canyon in which are nestled over a hundred tents of various sizes and descriptions, all full of seaside loafers. . . . The occupants of these portable dwellings are on the most friendly terms . . . neighborly borrowings of frying pans, tin cups and flea powder are carried on with the utmost good feeling . . . [The campers] evidently experienced a serene enjoyment in cutting loose from the comforts and luxuries of civilized life. . . . The time thus snatched from housekeeping and business is employed in bathing, fishing, gathering mosses and visiting.[20]

These campers and other leisure-seekers found their way to the canyon via stages offering regular service, following the old Indian trial that traversed the seventeen miles from Los Angeles. On Sundays, one contemporary visitor noted, about 600 to 700 people came from Los Angeles to enjoy the rustic setting and frolic on the beach. A new tie between Santa Monica and Los Angeles was thus formed as Santa Monica began to develop into a beachside backyard for the growing city.

While tourists enjoyed themselves a great deal in Santa Monica in the 1860s and 1870s, life was less carefree for Santa Monica's ranching families. It wasn't the tourists themselves that were causing the problems, but rather a host of economic problems that began plaguing the ranchers almost from the moment American rule began. To begin with, Americans had different rules about property than the Mexicans. Specifically the Land Grant Act of 1851 required Californio ranch owners to secure title to their land via American authorities. This was a lengthy process, and as long as it remained unfinished ranch owners could not claim to have clear title to their land. Of the Santa Monica area ranches, the owners of La Ballona were the first to have their title verified—but not until 1873. Meanwhile it took until 1882 for Rancho San Vicente y Santa Monica to receive its patent, and another year before ownership of Rancho Boca de Santa Monica was fully clarified.

This uncertainty might not have meant much to the ranchers if the cattle business had been going well, but it wasn't. By the 1860s the flush times of the Gold Rush were over. Santa Monica saw very heavy rains in 1861, followed by devastating droughts in 1862 and 1864. In these bleak years between one million and three million cattle perished in the "Cow Counties" of Southern California. To make things worse in Santa Monica, a smallpox epidemic killed Ysidro Reyes in 1861 (Francisco Marquez died earlier in 1850), leaving Rancho Boca de Santa Monica without its leading spokesman. With their cattle dying, ranch owners were still obliged to conform to another aspect of American life—paying taxes on their property. Land rich, but increasingly cash poor, the old Californio families often had little choice but to sell their lands (at low prices since title could not be assured) to meet their expenses.

Santa Monica was, of course, attractive to outsiders. The tourist trade in the canyon had already offered a glimpse of what an agreeable place it was, and what a mild climate it offered. The potential for agriculture or continued ranching was clear.

When all this could be bought at bargain basement prices, the Americans who were increasingly streaming into the area did not miss the chance.

One man with money to spend, and a hankering for Santa Monica, was Colonel Robert S. Baker. Baker was a Rhode Islander who came to California to get rich in the Gold Rush. But rather than prospecting for gold, Baker went into the business of supplying miners in San Francisco. From there he went on to become a prosperous sheep rancher in Northern California and on the Tejon Ranch in Kern County. It was with sheep ranching in mind that Baker eyed the Santa Monica area on a visit in 1872. Soon after, he convinced the cash-strapped Sepúlveda heirs of Rancho San Vicente y Santa Monica to sell him the entire place, all 30,260 acres, for about $55,000. Baker then acquired more acreage from Maria Antonia Villa de Reyes in 1873 when she agreed to part with about 2,000 acres of Rancho Boca de Santa Monica for the sum of $6,000. (The Marquez family retained its share of the rancho for the time being and has kept some of it to this day. Indeed Marquez descendants continue to live in the canyon and a private family cemetery located on San Lorenzo Street bears witness to the family's long residence there.) Baker's holdings were further rounded out with the purchase of 160 acres of Rancho La Ballona from the Machado family.

With these real estate deals Baker gained control of all the land that would become the city of Santa Monica. (When Baker married Arcadia Bandini in 1875, the two became a true power couple in Southern California real estate. Arcadia controlled vast tracts of Southern California land inherited both from her father, the prominent Californio Juan Bandini, and her deceased first husband, Abel Stearns.) In the course of only a few years in the 1870s, the land that would make up the city of Santa Monica passed from Californio to American hands.

Whatever Baker may have initially thought, Santa Monica was not destined for sheep ranching. It wasn't long before Baker, allied with a well-known surveyor and land promoter named Edward F. Beale, were envisioning a new city called "Truxton" (after Beale's son), which they would link by railroad to Los Angeles. Truxton, of course, never happened but the idea of a port city linked by rail to other commercial centers was a compelling one to another man who fancied the area—Senator John Percival Jones of Nevada. With Baker's help, Jones would see this vision through.

By the late 1800s Santa Monica had already been possessed and inhabited by three different groups—the Gabrielino, the Spanish, and the Californios—each with their own worldviews, reasons for being there, and designs on the land. Now something entirely new was on the horizon—a boomtown. Soon enough Santa Monica would be transformed into a place in which the American passions for get-rich-quick schemes, solid middle-class respectability, and progress with a capital "P" could be realized. In the process, the Californios, once so dominant and successful, would be pushed to the margins of society. Like the native people before them who had also been displaced, some of the old families remained in Santa Monica and continued with their accustomed ways. A few even continued to be influential in civic affairs. But their heyday was clearly over.

Chapter Four

A BOOMTOWN IS BORN

Santa Monica's history in the last three decades of the nineteenth century was like nothing that had come before. From a place of purely local interest—of concern to its residents and hardly anyone else—Santa Monica was, almost overnight, thrust into a role in a much bigger drama. From the 1870s until the turn of the twentieth century, Santa Monica attracted the attention of some of America's greatest oligarchs and was treated by them as a pawn in a high-stakes game over who would control transportation and shipping in and out of Southern California. Over these tumultuous decades Santa Monica's fortunes rose when investors and land speculators (particularly one John Percival Jones) tried to make the area into a major seaport and railroad terminus. But by the late 1870s this plan had gone bust and the fledgling town was cast adrift—a city in search of a purpose. Then, after weathering a bleak time, the town began to rise again like a phoenix from the ashes when Collis Huntington—the great railroad magnate—decided it suited his purposes to create a deep-water harbor with railroad facilities just north of the town. Years of turbulent wrangling over Huntington's plans, both locally and in Washington D.C., ended in 1897 when this project also failed and Santa Monica's hopes for greatness as a major seaport were once again dashed. Through it all Santa Monica was a microcosm for trends that were reshaping the West generally. Land booms and busts, railroad development, financial panics, the clashing wills of powerful tycoons, schemes to corner markets—Santa Monica saw it all as Americans attempted to turn their dreams into reality in this once quiet corner of Southern California.

In the early 1870s Robert S. Baker acquired the property that makes up Santa Monica today from members of the area's old Californio ranching families. Before long he began to see the possibilities for a town and railroad on the site, but his plan to build a place called "Truxton" never got off the drawing board. The idea did not die though. Instead it was brought to fruition by John Percival Jones, a U.S. Senator from Nevada. Indeed, not long after Baker had acquired his Santa Monica ranchlands, he decided to sell three quarters of his holdings to Senator Jones for about $160,000 (the remaining quarter he sold to his wife, Arcadia, for another $50,000).

Why would a senator from the state of Nevada want to buy most of Santa Monica? John P. Jones had some extremely good reasons. Jones was born in England and came to the United States as a baby. His parents had settled in Cleveland, Ohio and Jones, like many other immigrants, absorbed the pioneer atmosphere and sense of possibility in the wide-open West. Before long, his ambition brought him to California and then, later, to Nevada where vast fortunes were being made in the silver mines of the Comstock Lode. Indeed, this area held one of the richest silver veins in the world, and in 1859, twenty years following its discovery, it yielded over $300 million of the metal. Working as the superintendent and part owner of the fabulously productive Crown Point Mine, Jones himself became very wealthy. His fortune assured, Jones turned his hand to politics in the new state of Nevada and was elected to the U.S. Senate in 1873. But however rich and powerful Jones was, his ambitions were greater, which is how Santa Monica comes into the picture.

The late nineteenth century was a time of great railroad development in America. The first transcontinental railroad had been completed in 1869 and entrepreneurial men everywhere could see that railroads were the wave of the future, as well as a potentially lucrative source of profits and power for those who controlled them. California, with its lack of navigable rivers and remoteness from the rest of the United States, was particularly well suited to railroad development. Jones grasped these facts and devised his own plan to control the prosperous mining areas of Cerro Gordo (in the Inyo Mountains) and Panamint (nearby, on the edge of Death Valley) by building a supply railroad from Independence in the Owens Valley, through the Cajon Pass and down to San Bernardino. From there he planned to extend the rail line—what he dubbed the Los Angeles & Independence Railroad—all the way to the ocean at Santa Monica, where he would build a major seaport and city. The port would, he hoped, eventually supercede the area's long-used harbor at San Pedro, and Santa Monica would displace Los Angeles as the major urban center of Southern California. For conceiving and implementing these grandiose plans, Jones has earned a place in history as the father of modern Santa Monica. But Jones's plans were never really just about Santa Monica. Instead, they were part of an elaborate scheme with much larger goals than the simple building of a city.

Indeed, besides controlling mines near the Nevada border, Jones's plans challenged the dominance of one of the great powers in California at the time—the Southern Pacific Railroad—with ramifications for the Los Angeles area as well. The Southern Pacific had a stranglehold on the region thanks to its ownership of the Los Angeles & San Pedro Railroad, the only railroad serving Los Angeles and its port. (In 1876, the Southern Pacific's dominance in Southern California was further strengthened when the company completed tracks between San Francisco and Los Angeles, linking Los Angeles to transcontinental routes.) With a monopoly over rail transport in the region, the Southern Pacific charged whatever it wanted, and what it wanted was often exorbitant. Jones's railroad and new port threatened the Southern Pacific because it would offer a new way to move goods and people in and out of the region. Indeed, Jones's long-range plan for the railroad was to eventually extend it from Independence to Salt Lake City, where it would meet up with a transcontinental line and thus give Southern Californians freedom from the Southern Pacific's price gouging. In fact, it was this challenge to the Southern Pacific that attracted another legendary railroad magnate's attention to Jones's project. Jay Gould saw the Los

Angeles & Independence Railroad as a potentially useful pawn in his struggle for power with his arch-rival Huntington and, for a time, considered investing in it.

Though Gould took time to make up his mind, Jones did not wait to implement his ambitious plans. Soon after buying the Santa Monica ranchlands from Robert Baker, Jones worked with Baker to lay out the town and have it registered as the Township of Santa Monica. The boundaries for this new town were Twenty-Sixth Street to the northeast, Railroad Avenue (later renamed Colorado) on the southeast, Montana Avenue to the northwest, and, of course, the Pacific Ocean to the southwest.

By February of 1875 construction of the Los Angeles & Independence (in which Baker also had a role on the board of directors) had begun, starting with construction of the wharf located at the foot of today's Colorado Avenue. When finished, this wharf reached 1,740 feet into the bay and was capable of handling traffic from large ocean-going vessels. As the wharf took shape, one hundred Chinese laborers, brought from San Francisco for the purpose of grading and laying the track, began their arduous task. Starting at the wharf, these Chinese crews worked towards Los Angeles and by October 17, 1875, had completed enough track for a maiden run as far as La Cienega. Spirits were high as the first passengers on the Los Angeles & Independence departed towards Santa Monica on flat railroad cars equipped with chairs for the passengers (at this early stage, ordinary passenger cars had not yet been delivered). By November 31, 1875, the fledgling railroad was completed to Los Angeles where a depot in high Victorian style had been constructed to accommodate the line's customers.

Of course no town can be successful without inhabitants so, amidst all this construction, Jones made sure that Santa Monica was well-advertised. In the summer of 1875 advertisements touting the town's virtues appeared in newspapers, not only in California but in more distant parts of the country as well. One ad that appeared in San Francisco's *Figaro* newspaper began by casting aspersion on San Pedro as a "harbor so defective as almost to be worthless," and then lavishly praised the new town of Santa Monica:

> That Santa Monica is to be the future city of Southern California will be readily conceded after an examination of its many advantages. . . . The terminus of two trans-continental roads. Twelve miles of beautiful beach for riding and driving. A soil of unexampled fertility. A site of unsurpassing beauty. The terminus of the Los Angeles and Independence Railroad. Commanding the trade of Panamint, Coso, and Cerro Gordo. Surrounded by 100,000 acres of land for Orange, Olive, and Lemon Orchards. Twelve miles from Los Angeles. A harbor where vessels can find shelter in any storm. Thirty feet of water at the wharf at low tide. Abundant water from living springs, artesian wells and ordinary wells. Streets and lots have a natural grade. Climate the most delightful in the world.

> To merchants desiring to commence business of any kind.
> To mechanics seeking to establish themselves in a thriving locality.
> To invalids looking for health and profit.
> To all who wish to make a safe and profitable investment.
> SANTA MONICA offers a most inviting opportunity.[21]

Ads such as these hit their mark. Since transcontinental rail service had come to San Francisco in 1869, 70,000 people were arriving in California every year, some as tourists and some ready to start a new life in the state. These newcomers wrote letters back to those in the East and Midwest telling of California's charms, attracting even more people enthusiastic about the region and convinced that railroads would transform the state and generate fortunes along the way. All this created what historian Carey McWilliams called a "bubble of expectation" in Southern California at around the time Santa Monica was being advertised. In older towns like Los Angeles and Santa Barbara, "picturesque cottages were torn down . . . to make way for the new buildings of the cities-to-be. Wharfs, railway terminals, hotels, warehouses, and churches began to spring up in anticipation of the boom everyone expected."[22] Santa Monica joined this trend, though it did not have many old structures to tear down, offering its amenities to the many eager newcomers looking for a sure bet in California.

With the wharf constructed, the railroad to Los Angeles well underway, and backers pumping up the place, the time was ripe to begin auctioning off the lots that would comprise Santa Monica. July 15, 1875 was the date selected to begin. General Ulysses S. Grant was President of the United States and elsewhere the nation was in the process of reconstruction after the Civil War. But in Santa Monica everything was fresh, new, and full of expectation. Jones did all he could to get people to Santa Monica that day. Wagons were hired to transport people from Los Angeles, a special ship came down from San Francisco carrying about 150 potential buyers, and many more arrived in private conveyances. In all about 2,000 people attended, prompting the *Los Angeles Daily Star* to exclaim that the auction "drew forth the largest crowd of people ever seen together in Southern California."[23] The crowd was accommodated by bleachers set up on the palisades at the foot of what is now Wilshire Boulevard.

Leaving nothing to chance, Jones also took the trouble of engaging Tom Fitch as master of ceremonies, aided by auctioneer Alfred W. Noyes. Fitch was experienced in land sales, a seasoned veteran of the real estate booms of the Midwest. He and a couple of other gifted hucksters would later be said to have "auctioned off most of Southern California."[24] For the moment, however, he was concerned only with Santa Monica and poured all his effort into inspiring the crowd to trade their money for a piece of what he called "the Zenith of the Sunset Sea." Fitch promised that what was for sale was no less than:

> the Pacific ocean, draped with a sky of scarlet and gold…a southern
> horizon, rimmed with a choice collection of purple mountains, carved

in castles and turrets and domes . . . a frostless, bracing, yet unlanguid air, braided in with sunshine and odored with the breath of flowers.[25]

All of Jones's advance preparation, along with Fitch's honeyed words, produced a smashing success that day. With Noyes running the actual auction from a wooden stage, the crowd did not leave before spending more that $40,000 on Santa Monica land. The first lot sold was an attractive parcel, located at the corner of Ocean Avenue and Utah (later renamed Broadway). The second sale was to Harris Newmark, a prominent Jewish wool merchant from Los Angeles, who bought five lots on Ocean between Utah and Oregon (later renamed Santa Monica Boulevard) for $300 a piece. Indeed, members of Los Angeles's Jewish community participated actively in the first day of the auction, with four other Jewish families buying lots as well. The following day was even more successful with $43,000 in receipts. Indeed prices never dropped below $75 per lot, to the disappointment of bargain hunters. The enthusiasm of these first buyers inspired others to purchase a stake in the new town and lots sold briskly over the next few months.

Almost immediately after these early sales, a boomtown took shape on the lands previously given over almost exclusively to sheep and cattle. By late November, only four months after the first lots were sold, the *Outlook* newspaper reported that:

> Santa Monica continues to advance. We now have a wharf where Panama steamers have landed; a railroad completed to Los Angeles, a telegraph station, a newspaper, a post office, two hotels, one handsome clubhouse, several lodging houses, eight restaurants, a number of saloons, four groceries, three dry goods stores, two hardware stores, three fruit stores, one wool commission house, one news depot and bookstore, one bakery, one jewelry and watchmaker, one boot and shoe shop, two livery stables, one dressmaker, two tin shops, several contractors and builders, three real estate agencies, one insurance agency, one coal yard, one brick yard, two lumber yards, two private schools, and in a short time we shall have two churches and a public school.[26]

Only nine months after the land auction, Santa Monica already had a population of 1,000 living in about a hundred hastily-constructed houses and seventy-five tents. Newcomers continued to arrive daily thanks to special Los Angeles & Independence excursion trains that brought passengers to Santa Monica for $1 and encouraged them to spend the day enjoying seaside pleasures and soaking up the town's optimistic mood. After a couple of hundred years of extremely slow growth, 1875 was truly a time of stunning change for the Santa Monica area. For Jones, Baker, and the hundreds of others who now held an interest in the success of Santa Monica, the future looked bright indeed.

But success would not come that easily, despite this early promise. To begin with, the Southern Pacific and the men who ran it, especially Collis Huntington, had no intention of letting Santa Monica interfere with their lucrative monopoly in Southern California. Though Huntington and his associates did not mind seeing Jones spend a million dollars of his own money to build the Los Angeles & Independence Railroad, almost the minute its tracks reached Los Angeles, the Southern Pacific set to putting it out of business. By November of 1875 the Southern Pacific had cut passenger fares and freight rates to rock bottom for the trip between San Pedro and Los Angeles. Angelinos were pleased—at last the Southern Pacific wasn't gouging them—but for Jones and the Los Angeles & Independence Railroad, this cut-throat competition was killing. Moreover, Huntington put pressure on shipping companies that depended on the Southern Pacific for access to areas beyond Los Angeles to avoid Santa Monica in favor of San Pedro. Since at this stage Jones could only offer clients service to Los Angeles, his railroad was at a great disadvantage.

Jones's great wealth protected his railroad and the fledgling town for a time. But unfolding events soon tied his hands. To begin with, his efforts to secure investment funds from Jay Gould never came to fruition. Gould decided that he did not need Santa Monica as a pawn in his national rivalry with Huntington and his associates. Even worse, by the time Gould lost interest, Jones had gone broke. In a scenario repeated thousands of times in the nineteenth-century West, Comstock Lode stocks, once so lucrative, went bust. Jones, who was heavily invested there, felt the brunt of this crash amidst news that his Panamint investments had also gone sour. Meanwhile, by early 1876, a depression, generated in part by the Comstock crash and the bank failures that occurred in its wake, was weakening the economic climate in California generally. As times got tough the Los Angeles & Independence Railroad was forced to reduce service, which in turn reduced traffic on the line, which inevitably led to even greater deterioration in service.

Unable to keep the railroad running, Jones was forced to put the Los Angeles & Independence up for sale. Not surprisingly, however, buyers for a railroad that looked doomed to fail were scarce. By 1877 Jones was reduced to selling his railroad, for only $250,000, to the very operation that had driven him out of business—Collis Huntington and the Southern Pacific. Senator Jones, who once declared that he would "ruin Wilmington" (San Pedro) and that "Santa Monica, not Los Angeles is the logical metropolitan center of California," had to eat his words.[27] Of course Huntington did not really need the little Los Angeles & Independence Railroad. In fact, Huntington's partners at the Southern Pacific opposed the purchase. But Huntington, always masterful at manipulating power and influence, wanted to keep Jones friendly. After all, Jones was a U.S. senator whose vote might help Huntington in the future.

The fact that Huntington and the Southern Pacific had little use for the Los Angeles & Independence itself was soon made plain. The line's ornate Los Angeles station was closed and sold. The last ship docked at Jones's wharf in 1878 and not long afterwards Southern Pacific engineers declared it unsafe and arranged to tear almost all of it down, thereby removing the threat of any seagoing vessels depositing passengers or wares there. (Predictably, the Southern Pacific then raised freight and passenger rates to their former exorbitant levels from San Pedro to Los Angeles.) The Southern Pacific did leave the Los Angeles & Independence tracks intact however. They were useful for running two trains per day from Los Angeles to Santa Monica, with an extra train on Sundays to handle crowds of beachgoers. Thus by 1879 Santa Monica had been stripped of its original *raison d'être*. Its destiny as a major seaport and principal city of Southern California now looked like little more than a fanciful dream.

In a couple of short years Santa Monica had been transformed from a sparsely inhabited cattle ranch into a boomtown. But with the failure of Jones's grand plans, Santa Monica hit the skids just as quickly, and the late 1870s and early to mid-1880s were a bleak time for the town. Without shipping and the railroad there wasn't much to justify living in Santa Monica or starting businesses there, nor much to support the robust land prices of 1875 and 1876. Making things more difficult was the serious financial instability that was affecting California and the nation in these years. Not surprisingly then, many of the enterprises that had sprung up in the boomtown folded just as quickly, property values slumped, and the population dropped from 1,000 to only 350. The only bright spot was in the town's (and nearby Santa Monica Canyon's) continued attractiveness as a beach resort.

The dream of Santa Monica as a major seaport and important regional city seemed quite dead. No one could have predicted that it would come roaring back in the late 1880s, revived by the unlikeliest of men—Collis Huntington. Just as he had dashed Santa Monica's ambitions when they conflicted with his own in the 1870s, Huntington was more than willing to boost the town when it meshed with his own schemes to maintain the Southern Pacific's dominance of railroading in the West in the 1880s. And once Huntington, one of the most powerful men in America, had set his eye on little Santa Monica, it was thrust into the national spotlight, becoming part of an intense debate both locally and in Washington D.C. that would last for years.

It all started because the Los Angeles area was growing substantially in the late 1880s. After the Santa Fe Railroad arrived in the Los Angeles Basin in 1885, a fare war broke out between it and the Southern Pacific. (Just as Huntington and his associates had driven the Los Angeles & Independence Railroad out of business by cutting fares, Huntington hoped to undermine the Santa Fe's foothold in Southern California via cut-throat competition.) The result was a bonanza for passengers. A typical fare from the Missouri Valley to Southern California had been about $125. After the Santa Fe came, it dropped to $100 and continued to go down as each railroad undercut the other. By March of 1887, the Santa Fe and Southern Pacific were both offering a $12 fare, which then fell to $8, then $6, then $4, and finally $1 for passage across more than half the continent. The result was a huge influx of people who might never otherwise have had the means to come to California. In 1887 alone the Southern Pacific brought 120,000 people to Los Angeles while the Santa Fe had several trains a day steaming in from the east. All these people needed places to live and so, between

1887 and 1889, over sixty new towns were laid out in Southern California, covering almost 80,000 acres.

What all this population growth and building meant was that the Los Angeles area needed a better port. San Pedro had been operating since the earliest days of the pueblo, but the harbor there was shallow, the piers in poor condition, and the facilities generally primitive. Improving San Pedro to meet Los Angeles's growing needs would require a large investment to dredge the harbor and construct a breakwater, among other things. The federal government recognized the need for a deep-water port in the Los Angeles area and, by 1890, had appropriated funds to begin selecting the site and planning the project. Because San Pedro was the long-standing port of Los Angeles, it was the likely location for these federally-sponsored improvements. Indeed, by 1891 a final report to Congress (one of many "final" reports, it would turn out) on the location of the proposed deep-water port pointed to San Pedro as superior to other possible locations.

But the redoubtable Collis Huntington had different ideas. Huntington quickly grasped that if San Pedro was improved with federal money, it would likely be opened to other railroads and the Southern Pacific's monopoly over rail transportation in the region would be no more. Moreover, the Southern Pacific would have no way of preventing other railroads from accessing San Pedro as there were many possible approaches to the harbor. With these vexing possibilities looming, Huntington came up with a masterful plan to retain the Southern Pacific's stranglehold on Southern California, while at the same time benefiting from any expenditures the federal government might make developing a harbor. Santa Monica was the solution. If Huntington could convince the federal government to build its deep-water port at Santa Monica instead of San Pedro, the Southern Pacific's domination would be secure.

Santa Monica appealed to the shrewd Huntington because it had naturally restricted access to the sea. The beach was backed by cliffs, and railroads could reach the sea only through one narrow canyon (where Jones had previously built his railroad). All Huntington had to do to ensure the Southern Pacific would have sole access to any port at Santa Monica was to control this restricted passage and the beach frontage around it. That way no competitors to the Southern Pacific could ever elbow their way in.

Huntington lost no time in implementing this audacious plan. Indeed, even before publicly announcing his interest in promoting Santa Monica as a deep-water harbor, a subsidiary of Southern Pacific reached an agreement with members of the Marquez family, who still owned some beach frontage at Santa Monica Canyon, to gain rights of way. Meanwhile, Huntington met with his former rival, Senator Jones, and agreed to buy a quarter interest in Jones's Santa Monica property for $125,000. (Whatever animosity Jones may have felt for Huntington, as a major landholder Jones was savvy enough to see the profits he could make if Huntington succeeded in making the town into a major regional port.) Huntington also sent two agents to Santa Monica—Abbott Robinson and Fred Davis—with instructions to buy up more land in the area.

Having reached an agreement with Jones and having secretly bought other lands, it remained for Huntington to reach an accord with the only other major landholders in Santa Monica, Colonel Baker and his wife Arcadia Bandini de Baker. They too may have appreciated the rise in real estate values that would come if Huntington succeeded in making Santa Monica into a railroad and shipping hub, or perhaps they simply saw Huntington's plan as a way to revive the town they had helped found. In any case, they agreed to support him in his effort to make Santa Monica a world-class port. With these agreements in place, as the *New York World* newspaper reported on June 26, 1894, "Mr. Huntington's Santa Monica enterprise throughout its entire extent is as exclusive as though it were surrounded by a Chinese Wall."[28] No railroad, except the Southern Pacific, would ever be able to get into Santa Monica.

These advance preparations completed, Huntington went public with his Santa Monica idea. In 1891 the Southern Pacific announced that it was transferring its operations to Santa Monica, which it expected to become Los Angeles's principal port. When Huntington himself explained this to the Senate Commerce Committee in 1892, they immediately halted an appropriation of $250,000 for improving the port at San Pedro (evidence of Huntington's substantial political influence) and the battle was on. From this date until 1896, when the federal government decided definitively in favor of San Pedro, backers of San Pedro faced off against Huntington and his influential friends, both locally and in Washington D.C., as each sought to steer federal monies their own way.

Of course, it was not only Huntington who had a stake in the outcome. All of Southern California watched the battle, and many justifiably feared a decision in favor of Santa Monica because it would absolutely assure the Southern Pacific's oppressive grip on the region. Santa Monicans, for their part, had reasons to be enthusiastic about Huntington's plans. Santa Monica had recovered somewhat from its disappointment after Jones's wharf and railroad failed. By the late 1880s Santa Monica, like the rest of the Los Angeles area, was enjoying another land boom that brought more people to town and raised real estate prices. An auction of Santa Monica lots held in May of 1887 brought in $42,000 from enthusiastic buyers and shortly after, even though prices were climbing dramatically, lots continued to sell briskly. But the American economy (not to mention the Southern California real estate market) was very volatile in these years. By 1893 a massive financial panic was engulfing the nation, resulting in a serious depression that was at its worst in 1893 and 1894. In the face of all this economic turbulence, Huntington's plan offered Santa Monicans the chance at a solid economic base for their town that might sustain livelihoods and prosperity over the long run.

The views and hopes of Santa Monicans were, however, largely inconsequential in this saga. Officials in Washington D.C. would determine whether San Pedro or Santa Monica would be favored and so Huntington quickly set about establishing "facts on the ground" that would sway these decision-makers. To do this, and thereby maintain the Southern Pacific's monopoly, was so important to Huntington that he was willing to build a new world-class wharf and railroad facilities himself, the better to show off Santa Monica's promise. To this end, the Southern Pacific sent surveyors to Santa Monica in 1891, and by 1892 workers had begun digging out a tunnel at Ocean Avenue and Colorado. Meanwhile, tracks were laid from there to a point north of Santa Monica Canyon where a mammoth wharf would be constructed. This wharf site, two miles north of the town limits, was appealing both for engineering reasons involving ocean currents, and because it required trains to travel along the base of Santa Monica's palisades where the Southern Pacific had exclusive right-of-way.

The wharf itself was the centerpiece of Huntington's ambitious plan and when it was completed in October of 1893 it was, indeed, a remarkable structure. Officially named Port Los Angeles by Huntington in 1893 (but also known simply as the Long Wharf), it extended an exceptional 4,720 feet into the bay and was equipped for heavy traffic from seagoing vessels and the trains that would serve them. The sea end of the wharf boasted seven sets of tracks, a massive coal bunker with a capacity of 80,000 tons, and a depot with a waiting room, a post office, offices, and sleeping space for employees, as well as a restaurant open to the public. Even as controversy swirled around Huntington's plan and lawmakers in Washington wrangled about whether San Pedro or Santa Monica would be the recipient of federal expenditures, Port Los Angeles began to function as a major regional shipping center. The *San Mateo* was the first vessel to use the wharf, arriving from San Francisco in May of 1893 carrying 4,200 tons of coal as well as passengers. In the years between 1893 and 1896 a total of 759 ships, both foreign and American, used the wharf.

For a time, Port Los Angeles seemed to be living up to its billing as Huntington did all he could to promote Santa Monica as Southern California's best choice for a deep-water harbor. But the truth was that the whole project was a great gamble. In the years that Port Los Angeles was built and operated, the harbor debate never stopped raging and, in the end, when the decision came down, San Pedro was the winner. On March 1, 1897, a blue-ribbon board of engineers declared that San Pedro was, without a doubt, the superior site for a deep-water port. Those in favor of a "free harbor" had won and all of Huntington's political influence and money could not change the result. There was dancing in the streets in Los Angeles, but at Santa Monica hopes for greatness had been dashed once again.

Collis Huntington died in 1900 and in the decade that followed Port Los Angeles slowly declined. Though still used for a time by passenger steamers shuttling up and down the coast between San Francisco and Los Angeles, as well as by some ships delivering lumber and other materials, the new management at Southern Pacific allowed the wharf to deteriorate. By 1908 Southern Pacific had lost all interest in the facility and leased it to the Los Angeles Pacific Company. This precursor to the Pacific Electric Company ran electric trolley cars out on the wharf as part of its "Balloon Route" from Los Angeles. Advertised as "an ocean voyage on wheels," tourists thrilled to the feeling of gliding out over the deep blue sea. But this light use was, of course, a far cry from what the wharf had been built to do. After being partially torn down in 1913 (its depot and coal bunker were dismantled and the wharf was shortened), the wharf continued as a tourist attraction and fishing spot until 1920. Then even the trolley line abandoned the route in the face of prohibitive maintenance costs, and the remaining length of wharf was destroyed. Only twenty-seven years after Port Los Angeles was born, almost all vestiges of Huntington's once great plan to remake Santa Monica were gone.

Senator John P. Jones and Collis Huntington were alike in many ways. Both were wealthy. Both made fortunes in typically nineteenth-century endeavors. Both were powerful men who dreamt big, hatched ambitious plans, and implemented them with fierce determination. But both men failed to turn Santa Monica into an important railroad hub and port. That both Jones and Huntington failed does not make them irrelevant to Santa Monica's history. On the contrary, their failure was pivotal for Santa Monica. Had Jones or Huntington succeeded, Santa Monica would be a very different place today than it is. Not only that, their story is emblematic of a thousand other attempts, some successful and some not, by Americans to remake the West according to the American precepts of progress, entrepreneurship, and bold action. These values, flung up against the vast canvas of the West, transformed Southern California in the late nineteenth century and made it a truly different kind of place than it had been under Mexican or Spanish rule.

Though Santa Monica did not become a major transportation hub or port, the town Jones started and Huntington furthered took root and eventually flourished on its own terms. Despite the failures and the recurring boom and bust cycles that characterized the era, the town endured. Once development of this former cattle ranch had begun, there would be no turning back. Indeed, while Senator Jones's and later Collis Huntington's railroad dramas unfolded, the town residents were busy refining city government, founding churches, establishing schools, running businesses, and devising all manner of civic organizations. From 1875 until the turn of the twentieth century Santa Monica evolved from a dusty frontier town to a settled township. As more and more people flocked to Southern California in the decades after 1875, Santa Monica was in a position to reinvent itself—in ways that its entrepreneurial backers hadn't envisioned—to capitalize on the hopes and wishes of these newcomers. In the process, the town would emerge as something richer and more interesting than a one-note transportation hub. The development of a diverse population, the pursuit of health and leisure, and the embrace of an increasingly powerful neighbor—Los Angeles—would all help to shape Santa Monica as it found a niche for itself and a distinct character of its own by the early twentieth century.

Chapter Five

THE NEW CITY AND ITS PEOPLE

Though Santa Monica was initially conceived as a railroad terminus and port, ironically the failure of such schemes did not mean the failure of Santa Monica itself. On the contrary, even as Jones's and Huntington's railroad plans played out in the late nineteenth century, Santa Monica was in the process of finding a more natural niche for itself—one in which leisure and tourism would play key roles. But there was more to Santa Monica than that. Between 1875 and the 1920s, the town grew into a city with all the institutions urban dwellers need, from a police force to churches and clubs, promoting everything from women's suffrage to art appreciation. In the process the city's residents created a workable government, wrestled with moral problems, and forged social bonds. And just as civic life was multifaceted, so was the city's population. Reflecting the dynamism of Southern California in this era, Santa Monica was home not only to white Americans but also to communities of African Americans, Chinese, Hispanics (whether the old Californios, or new Mexican immigrants), Japanese, and Jews, as well as immigrants from other lands. In its first fifty years, Santa Monica was indeed a crossroads where Americans and people from the far corners of the world met, all contributing to make Santa Monica a desirable destination.

In early 1875 Santa Monica was little more than a name attached to mostly undeveloped ranch lands. Soon after the first lots were sold, houses began to sprout up quickly and a community was born. Much remained to be done, however, to make Santa Monica a serviceable town and, in the years that followed, the inhabitants poured their energy into all manner of civic projects. To begin with, there was the problem of town governance. In 1875 the town's founders had registered Santa Monica's birth with Los Angeles County, but as an unincorporated area Santa Monica did not have the privileges of self-government. By 1880, however, the population of the Santa Monica area had grown to 417, and by 1886 some among this group were ambitious individuals who wished to see Santa Monica incorporated. Although the townspeople were ready to vote on the issue by the spring of 1886, the way the election was carried out revealed a certain civic immaturity. As one account explained:

> The first election resulted in defeat for incorporation by one vote.
> The count showed the majority first for one side and then for the
> other and the result was a tie until the last vote was counted. The

last vote was "no," much to the disappointment and indignation of the corporators.

The promoters of the election provided a printed ballot to vote for incorporation, but none to vote against it, and announced when written ballots against incorporation were offered, that they would not be counted.

As there was no printing office in Santa Monica and no organized opposition, it was some time in the afternoon, after a trip had been made to Los Angeles, before "no" ballots were obtained.

There was much indignation at what was considered a political trick to disfranchise them, and those opposed to incorporation in a few hours mustered sufficient votes to defeat it. In fact this was really the cause of defeat.[29]

Apparently some of the overeager proponents of incorporation were those who thought it might benefit them financially. J.W. Scott, for one, had just finished constructing the enormous Arcadia Hotel and bathhouse on the beach and hoped a new city government would levy a $1,000 fee on any other new bathhouses, thereby protecting his enterprise from competition. Others local entrepreneurs looked forward to the business licenses and franchises a new city could grant that might give them special advantages. On the other hand, those against incorporation seem also to have had financial motivations. They feared a city government would cost too much.

Whatever the motivations of inhabitants, proponents soon organized another election, held November 30, 1886, and this time they prevailed by a vote of 96 to 71. The city now officially became, in the nomenclature of California municipalities, a sixth-class city. Incorporation put local decisions into the hands of Santa Monicans themselves and the first elected officials, a board of five trustees charged with running the city, lost no time in setting down laws to improve and regulate the life of the community. At their first meeting, held in December, these trustees—John Steere, Dr. E.C. Folsom, A.E. Ladd, William S. Vawter, and the aforementioned J.W. Scott—began by appointing various city officials as well as a marshal to keep order in the city.

With these basics in place, the trustees turned their attention to what they must have considered the city's most pressing problems. Addressing moral issues was high on their agenda. Their first ordinance, adopted in January of 1887, made it clear that anyone keeping a disorderly house or engaging in disorderly conduct would be punished by a fine or time in the as-yet-unbuilt city jail. Other early ordinances prohibited "houses of prostitution and ill-fame," and made vagrancy (that included the activities of "common prostitutes and drunkards" as well as those who were simply beggars or idle persons) illegal.

Besides these issues of vice, the trustees also dealt with improving the physical quality of life in Santa Monica. The trustees established a "street poll tax" of $2 on all male inhabitants of the city to provide funds for improvement of the city's thoroughfares. And they passed a measure prohibiting "the deposit of manure, garbage or refuse matter in the streets, alleys or other places," setting a $10 fine or ten days in jail as the penalty for violators. Overall, in the years after the city was first incorporated, city officials spent quite a bit of time responding to calls from residents to improve streets, build sidewalks, repair bridges, and otherwise make the city look more like a city and less like a dusty frontier town. Their efforts were successful enough that by 1898 one resident could report that, "I am sure that you would be surprised at the change in Santa Monica. No more must one wade knee-deep in dust while making his way to the beach, for the roads are nicely graded and the sidewalks cemented."[30]

Public safety was another concern for Santa Monica's late nineteenth-century leaders. To begin with, the trustees realized that a jail was needed to accommodate violators of the various ordinances they had passed and, in 1887, appropriated $600 for a combination jail and pound. In addition, they appointed a night watchman (paid partially by the city and partially by the city's businesspeople) by 1888. Ten years later, in 1898, the city hired its first full-time policeman. Police officers in these years spent much of their time rounding up drunks and carrying them by wheelbarrow to jail. As the city grew, however, a more elaborate police force was needed and by 1907 Santa Monica employed eight officers, including chief-of-police Max Barretto. Some things didn't change though as inebriates spilling out of Santa Monica's many saloons remained the mainstay of the police department's work. By the 1910s, it was time to upgrade police services once more and a new detective bureau was added, motorcycle officers took to the streets (to keep up with the growing number of motor vehicles in the city), and a call box system was installed that allowed residents to more easily summon officers.

Meanwhile, because fire was an ever-present threat to the wooden structures that made up much of the city, twenty fire hydrants were purchased by the city in 1888. In March of 1889 the Santa Monica Hose and Hook and Ladder Company, a volunteer fire brigade, organized to improve fire protection. These firefighters had 2,000 feet of hose, two horse-drawn hose carts, and a hook and ladder truck. This equipment was augmented in 1900 when the city funded a combination hose and chemical wagon and horses to pull it. By 1913 the fire department upgraded to motorized equipment.

While the city trustees initially held meetings at the Santa Monica Hotel, which stood at Colorado and Ocean Avenues, by 1903 an imposing official city hall at Fourth and Oregon (today's Santa Monica Boulevard) was open for business. As Santa Monica's civic life was becoming more complex, the form of city government evolved as well. 1906 was an important year for the city when voters agreed to be governed by a city charter, a move that allowed Santa Monicans much discretion in determining local affairs. The original charter provided for seven city council members (each elected from specific wards) and a mayor. However, because these council members were not full-time public servants, but rather businessmen who took on city responsibilities in addition to their ordinary jobs, city matters were not always dealt with promptly. Santa Monica's ever-growing population, which expanded from 417 in 1880 to 7,208 by 1905, and would reach 15,252 by 1920, made it increasingly obvious the city needed full-time officials. Thus, by 1915 the city's charter was rewritten to allow for three elected commissioners to run the city, a system that remained in place until after World War II.

City government was but one manifestation of the energy residents poured into making Santa Monica a viable city. Providing for religious worship was another top priority. Indeed, only months after the first town lots were sold in 1875, Santa Monica already had two organized churches. Very soon after the town was born, sisters Jennie and Emma Vawter were distressed by the lack of regard for the Sabbath in the new town. Taking matters into their own hands, the sisters organized a Union Sunday School, which met at the Vawter home beginning in September, 1875. This body helped inspire like-minded residents to form a Presbyterian church in Santa Monica, which was accomplished on September 28, 1875. The church consisted of twelve charter members, including the Vawters. By 1876 this First Presbyterian Church had constructed a building at Third and Arizona, on lots donated by town founders Senator Jones and Colonel Baker, and was well on its way to becoming a center of community activity. Meanwhile, a group of Methodists held its first meetings shortly after the town was founded in 1875 and quite swiftly incorporated as the Methodist Episcopal Church (now known as First United Methodist Church). Befitting a boomtown, these industrious Methodists managed to raise a chapel at the corner of Sixth and Arizona even before the year 1875 ended, setting in motion the church's role as a religious and social hub.

Santa Monicans were nothing if not diverse in their faith and the last decades of the nineteenth century saw other new churches spring up in profusion. Catholicism, of course, played a role in local history even before the town's founding, and there were enough adherents in the new town for mass to be celebrated in Santa Monica by 1887. Seven years later St. Monica's Church was established. The Baptists, meanwhile, organized a South Santa Monica Sunday School in 1890 and built a Baptist chapel in 1892. Members of this congregation later branched off to start Trinity Baptist Church in the northern part of the city. The Salvation Army brought its particular brand of religious activism to Santa Monica in 1893. Episcopalians organized regular services by 1885 and built St. Augustine-by-the-Sea Episcopal Church in 1887 on land donated for that purpose by Arcadia Bandini de Baker. In addition, the First Church of Christ, Scientist, Santa Monica organized in 1898, building the first Christian Scientist church on the West Coast at Seventh and Oregon (now Santa Monica Boulevard) in 1900.

Church building did not end in 1900. Many new congregations were organized in the early decades of the twentieth century. Notable among them were several churches serving Santa Monica's small but growing African-American population.

The earliest of these was the Colored Methodist Episcopal Church (now known as the Christian Methodist Episcopal Church), formed in 1908. Begun with a few members that met in Hull's Hall at Fourth and Bay Streets under the guidance of the Right Reverend Charles H. Phillips, their permanent home became the Phillips Chapel at 2001 Fourth Street. In 1920 a small group of African Americans met at a private home at Seventeenth Street and Broadway to found Calvary Baptist Church, which grew in influence over the following decades. Not long afterwards, Santa Monica's black population was large enough to sustain another church, the First African Methodist Episcopal Church. The city's Jewish population, for its part, enjoyed its first religious services in Santa Monica when Sabbath eve services were organized in 1912 at the Masonic Hall on Marine Street. However, it was not until 1939 that a permanent Jewish congregation, Beth Sholom Temple, was founded in the city.

Southern California in this era was a place where almost everyone was from somewhere else. In this situation of flux, newcomers were eager to construct familiar institutions, like churches, as well as establish organizations that could make it easier to identify like-minded people and express their own ideals and preferences. This urge to belong helps explain the explosion of clubs and associations founded during the city's formative decades. Among the first voluntary associations was the Santa Monica Woman's Christian Temperance Union, started in 1884. This organization worked to curb excessive liquor consumption, sought the enactment of prohibition laws, and agitated for women's suffrage and equal rights. In Santa Monica the WCTU also established the city's first library, a reading room opened in 1885, financed by donations from leading citizens. Fraternal organizations also took hold in early Santa Monica. In 1891 the first meeting of Masons took place and soon after Santa Monica Lodge 307 was founded. For a time these Masons met in the Santa Monica Bank building before moving into the Masonic Hall at Second and Santa Monica in 1916. The 1890s also saw the birth of the Santa Monica Order of the Eastern Star, Chapter 113, as well as an Odd Fellows Lodge. Politics also motivated residents to form the Santa Monica Democratic Club, active in the 1890s, as well as the Good Government League, begun in 1901 for the purpose of reforming city government.

The early decades of the twentieth century saw even more social bonding. By 1900 there was a Camera Club holding regular meetings. The Santa Monica Bay Women's Club organized in 1904. In the same year Santa Monica Lodge 906 of the Benevolent and Protective Order of Elks was born. Another fraternal organization spring into being in 1905, the Ocean Park Lodge of Masons. Not to be left out, Santa Monica's female descendants of Americans of the Revolutionary War period formed a local chapter of the Daughters of the American Revolution in 1906. Meanwhile, parents of school-age children banded together in a local PTA group by 1910, and some of their children found social camaraderie in the first Boy Scout troops, organized in 1917. People interested in science could join the Santa Monica Biological Club.

Even more organizations were formed in the 1920s, including the Rotary Club, the Lions Club, the Optimist Club, the Kiwanis Club, the YMCA, the Girl Scouts, and the Santa Monica Writers Club. As Charles S. Warren, who edited the *Outlook* newspaper in the early twentieth century pointed out, the average person could not "make his way through the world . . . without committees, clubs, leagues, societies, lodges and associations."[31] With these and scores of other groups not mentioned here, Santa Monicans proved Warren's point and demonstrated their commitment to creating a dense social fabric where none had existed before.

Schools, of course, were also necessary to the life of the city and city leaders quickly attended to their establishment. Santa Monica's first school opened to students in March of 1876 in the First Presbyterian Church with a teacher paid for by the city. Not long afterwards Santa Monica's trustees decided to build a two-story school building, which was funded at more than $4,200 via a property tax. Residents avoided having to buy the land, however, as city founders Senator Jones and Colonel Baker donated two lots on Sixth Street for the purpose. Though conceived as an elementary school, by 1891 high school courses were added to the Sixth Street School's curriculum. Other schools in the area included the Canyon School, begun in 1894 to serve inhabitants there, including descendants of the old Californio families, and Lincoln High School, constructed in 1897 at Tenth and Arizona. With Santa Monica's population increasing rapidly, the years between 1897 and 1915 were especially active as a total of eighteen new schools opened their doors to the city's young people. This number included a new high school, Santa Monica High, to replace Lincoln High. The site chosen was Prospect Hill, the school's present site, and building commenced in 1912. In the years that followed thousands of youngsters grew up in Santa Monica's public schools, hardly imagining the fact that only a few decades earlier neither schools nor city had even existed. Santa Monica Junior College (now Santa Monica College) added higher education to the city's amenities starting in 1929.

All these efforts to make the city come alive were reflected in another important institution of the time, the *Outlook* newspaper. Originally owned and managed by Kentuckian Lemuel Fisher, this newspaper began as a weekly in 1875 with some success. However, in the bleak years that followed the failure of Senator Jones's plan to turn Santa Monica into a major port and railroad terminus, the paper ceased publication. From 1878 until 1887 it remained shuttered. But once revived, the *Outlook* was indefatigable. By 1896 it was converted into a daily publication under the joint ownership of D.G. Holt and Robert C. Gillis, and changed its name to the *Daily Outlook* accordingly. In 1919 it changed its name again to the *Evening Outlook*. Whatever its name, the newspaper served as an important community forum, announcing events, stating opinions, advertising local businesses, and exerting an influence over many issues facing the city. Remarkably, this newspaper continued in this role through most of the twentieth century, only ceasing publication in 1998.

If institutions and organizations are the backbone of a city, people are its life blood. But who were the Santa Monicans making the city what it was in this era? A large segment consisted of white Americans who came from the East and Midwest, attracted by the promise of a new kind of life filled with sunshine and prosperity. While the Gold Rush had attracted many single fortune hunters of dubious background to California, white Americans who came to California in the 1880s and 1890s were generally families of comfortable means. As J.P. Widney wrote of Southern California in 1888, "One noteworthy feature of the incoming population is that it is made up almost entirely of the well-to-do—those who bring intelligence and money with them, and are prepared to improve their lands at once."[32] One nineteenth-century tourist book described Southern California's white pioneers further:

> The greatest number of them came from the stores, counting-houses, shops, and offices of their homes in the eastern states. Lawyers who had fled the stifling air of the courtroom, and the dusty tomes of their libraries; physicians; and others unused to manual toil, comprised almost altogether the people who here took upon themselves the labor and privations of founding a new community.[33]

The ample resources and education of Santa Monica's early white settlers helps explain how they were able to construct a city with a full complement of churches, schools, and other civic amenities in an amazingly short time after the town's founding.

White immigrants who came to Southern California after this first wave of affluent settlers, in the period from 1900 through the 1920s, tended to be less prosperous but still solidly middle-class. Their influence can be seen in the institutions of middle-class respectability that dominated Santa Monica's early social scene, including the numerous fraternal organizations and church groups, as well as in a push for public morality via prohibition of alcohol that preoccupied (and sometimes divided) the city for many years.

Whether wealthy or middle class, white immigrants came to Santa Monica in part because of well-crafted publicity campaigns promoting the region in the late nineteenth and early twentieth centuries. In the nineteenth century railroads did much of the advertising, hoping to increase use of their routes to the West. The Southern Pacific, for example, set special "land seeker" fares, organized excursion trains, sent lecturers to eastern towns to extol Southern California's virtues, and even sold lots in some communities. Meanwhile, local boosters such as Charles Lummis published magazines like *Land of Sunshine* that infused the region with a romantic identity, and books, with titles like *Of Oranges and Snowfields*, showed Americans that in Southern California flowers bloomed all winter, ripe fruit could be plucked from the trees, and a healthy and prosperous life was practically guaranteed. Individual cities also chimed in to attract newcomers. In Santa Monica civic boosters dreamed up slogans like "Santa Monica: Peach of all Beaches," and used them to draw attention to the city's merits.

White Americans responding to these calls to move west certainly dominated Southern California in the years after 1875, but they were far from the only inhabitants of the area. In Santa Monica, as in other areas across the state, the Californios—some of whose families dated back to the time of the founding of the missions—persisted. By the 1880s, most of California's old Hispanic families retained neither the great wealth nor the political power they had enjoyed earlier in the century, but they did continue their traditions. One 1888 photograph, for example, documents an annual May Day picnic hosted by the Marquez family. In it over fifty members of local Californio families, from babies to graybeards, are shown under the sycamores in Santa Monica Canyon. A couple of decades later festivities like this were still occurring. Joaquin de la Peña, a Marquez family descendant, recalled that, "When I was a kid—1911, 1912, 1913—all the Spanish families would gather in Santa Monica Canyon for a barbeque. We'd kill a couple of steers . . . two or three wooden barrels of beer . . . a three day celebration."[34] Just as in the days of the ranchos, de la Peña remembered, Spanish was spoken. Family milestones like weddings, baptisms, and funerals offered excuses for get-togethers, and the open-handed hospitality that had characterized life on the old Mexican ranches remained a key value. Indeed, the rancho tradition persists even today with the descendants of Francisco Marquez, one of the original owners of Rancho Boca de Santa Monica, who still live on a portion of the old land grant in Santa Monica Canyon.

Besides maintaining these traditions Californio descendants, in Santa Monica at least, succeeded in carving out active and important roles in the new city. Arcadia Bandini de Baker, a native Californian and wife of Colonel Robert Baker, was one Hispanic who had great influence in early Santa Monica. As a large landowner in the area, her actions affected the city's course. Her decision to join forces with Collis Huntington when he was trying to develop Santa Monica as Port Los Angeles is one example. As a wealthy philanthropist she encouraged the growth of churches and other institutions by bestowing land and money for their use. When Arcadia died in 1912, her obituary predicted that her funeral would be "the largest ever held in Los Angeles owing to the popularity of the old lady throughout Southern California."[35]

Juan Carrillo, scion of a Californio family once based in Los Angeles, was also notable for his influence in early Santa Monica. Carrillo moved to Santa Monica in 1881. He was elected a city trustee in 1888 and served until 1900, part of the time as president of the trustees and honorary mayor. Later he served the city as superintendent of streets.

Despite this vibrancy, it was nevertheless true that in the city of Santa Monica's formative years, the Hispanic element was largely a remnant of a past time. Californios were few in number and new immigrants from Mexico were even scarcer. (It has been estimated that there were only 8,000 Mexican-born persons living in the entire state in 1900.) It was not until heavy migration from Mexico began around 1910, driven both by poor economic conditions there and by the political upheavals of the Mexican Revolution, that the Hispanic community began to grow again. In Santa Monica, these newcomers would eventually congregate in the neighborhood bounded by Olympic and Pico Boulevards from Fourteenth to Twentieth Streets (called *La Veinte* by Hispanic residents) and add a unique element to the city's growing and diverse population.

African Americans also played a role in Santa Monica's formative years. Blacks had been present in Southern California since the earliest days of the Los Angeles pueblo, but their numbers were small. However, from only about 188 blacks in all of Los Angeles County in 1880, the population slowly but steadily grew over the ensuing decades. While racial discrimination was never absent from Southern California, the area was relatively hospitable to African Americans in the years from around 1900 until the 1920s. Aware of this fact, many came looking for a better life. In line with these trends, early twentieth-century records from Santa Monica indicate that a small black community was forming. As of 1907 a man named Gilbert McCarroll had opened Santa Monica's first black-owned business, a shoe-shine parlor. This early business failed but the city's African-American residents persisted. By the 1920s a small core of businesses such as the Dewdrop Inn at Second and Broadway, Thurman's Rest-A-While beach cottages, and Gilbert's Grocery and Soda Fountain (also owned by Gilbert McCarroll) had developed.

Unfortunately, due to racial discrimination most African Americans at the time were confined to domestic and service work. As James Maxwell, a black immigrant who arrived in Santa Monica in 1920, recalled, "When I came here . . . the only jobs my people did were laboring work—that's all. There weren't any professional trades or anything like that."[36] Moreover, the relatively good social and economic conditions that initially attracted blacks to the area in the late nineteenth and very early twentieth centuries deteriorated. By the 1920s increased anti-black prejudice and restrictive Jim Crow rules became daily facts of life for the city's black citizens. Though often not stated explicitly, African Americans knew from experience that they were unwelcome at many hotels, restaurants, theatres, and other establishments. Blacks were also barred from most of the city's beaches (as they were from Southern California beaches in general), with the exception of the beach located at the foot of Pico Boulevard, known informally among African Americans as the "Ink Well." Blacks who transgressed these boundaries faced hostility. Indeed, at an Armistice celebration after World War I a black man named Arthur Valentine took his family to a whites-only part of Santa Monica beach. White beachgoers called the authorities who attempted to force Valentine off the beach. When he resisted he was beaten, shot, and then arrested for disturbing the peace. A judge later threw out the charge but the point was nonetheless crystal clear—Santa Monica offered neither equality nor freedom to its black residents.

Excluded and discriminated against by the white community, black Santa Monicans nonetheless labored to create churches, clubs, and the other institutions that knit newcomers together and enriched their community. As such they founded their first church, the Colored Methodist Episcopal Church mentioned above, as well as Calvary Baptist Church in 1920 and the First African Methodist Episcopal Church in 1923. Black men established the Crescent Bay Masonic Lodge in 1911 and black women bonded in clubs such as the Philomathean Charity, Literary and Art Club, founded in 1921. Even in these early years of community building, Southern California blacks worked to improve their situation and break down the barriers erected by white society. For example, though blacks were often limited in housing choices due to racial covenants restricting them to certain areas, the NAACP was already at work in Southern California fighting these onerous restrictions. In Santa Monica, residents took action as well. Historian Delilah Beasley recorded the case of a black Santa Monican named C.E. Brunson, who succeeded in having an objectionable anti-black sign removed from the pier around 1919.

The Chinese were another significant element of Santa Monica's population in the city's formative years, reflecting their important place in California generally as laborers. Indeed, by the 1870s the Chinese were the largest foreign group in California, making up one tenth of the population and one fourth of the wage labor force. In 1880, in Southern California alone there were about 20,000 Chinese residents. Chinese men came to the state for several reasons: to make fortunes in the Gold Rush, to flee the war and poverty that ravaged southeast China at the time, and to build the Southern Pacific railroad. In Santa Monica it was the Chinese who graded the route and laid the tracks for the Los Angeles & Independence Railroad when it was constructed in 1875. After the railroads were largely completed, these hardworking but poorly paid Chinese men worked as field hands and as truck farmers, cultivating vegetables for sale in towns and cities. In Southern California, the Chinese established a virtual monopoly over the retail distribution of produce in the late nineteenth century. Les Storrs recalled that in early twentieth-century Santa Monica, Chinese produce men would drive through the alleys delivering their goods, "marking the bills in the paint on the corner of houses, to be paid later."[37] In addition, Carey McWilliams, a historian alive when these Chinese workers were still numerous, noted that, "When the tourist hotels began to appear throughout the region in the 1870s, Chinese were practically the only servants employed."[38] They were almost certainly employed in some of the many tourist establishments that flourished in Santa Monica in this era. Chinese men also operated laundries, did restaurant work, and were employed as cooks, houseboys, and servants in private homes. For example, Nancy Lucas, the nineteenth-century owner of much of the land that makes up Ocean Park today, is recorded as having been rather eccentric—in part because she lived alone in her large house with only her Chinese cook for company. These contributions have largely gone unheralded because Chinese laborers were at the bottom of the social hierarchy. As single men they did not generally found families that carried on their stories. Moreover, by the 1920s Southern California's Chinese population was already in decline. Still, in doing the menial labor that others wanted to avoid, in growing and distributing food, in manning the hotels that brought tourists to the region, these anonymous Chinese made an important contribution to the city in its early years.

The Japanese came to Santa Monica later than the Chinese, but they too were a visible element in the city's early days. While the Chinese lived and worked among other residents of the city, the Japanese initially lived apart, in a little village dedicated mostly to fishing located past Santa Monica Canyon on the north side of the Long Wharf. The village's founding member was Hatsuji Sano, who arrived at Port Los Angeles in 1899 and began leasing beach land from the Southern Pacific Railroad. Over time the village's population grew to about 300, all nestled at the base of the cliffs just next to the wharf in small wooden houses built on the sand. Despite the somewhat precarious beach location where winter tides sometimes inundated homes, there was even a small Methodist Mission in the village for those inclined to Christian worship. For schooling, however, children attended the Canyon School where they learned English and studied alongside other local kids. Exploiting the bounty of Santa Monica Bay and its environs, the village's thirty boats commonly pulled in thirty tons of fish a day of large species including tuna, yellowtail, and mackerel, as well as smaller fish. Much of their catch was then shipped from the Long Wharf via a special morning train to Los Angeles, in part for the delectation of Japanese living there who appreciated the freshness of the fish when preparing sashimi.

The village also served Los Angeles's Japanese community in another way, by providing a tourist getaway for successful merchants from Little Tokyo and for Japanese visiting from abroad. In 1909 a Japanese named Kiichiro Waseda is credited with establishing the first hotel to cater to Japanese in the area, the Rako Kan, located in Santa Monica Canyon. In 1911 Hatsuji Sano opened another inn located in the village itself, the Boyo Kan, advertising "clean rooms, excellent food, convenient for swimming, hot bath, etc."[39] Eventually there were at least three tourist inns in the village, as well as less attractive shacks built to house men working for the railroad. Aside from lodging, by 1914 there were movies being made in the village as well. Like other filmmakers attracted to Southern California during this era, Japanese companies brought Japanese actors to the village for filming and then sent the results to Japan to be enjoyed by moviegoers there. It was not unusual for costumed actors and bit players to stroll the Long Wharf during breaks in filming, providing an interesting spectacle for sailors and passengers whose ships tied up there.

Despite all these activities, this little village was not destined to last forever. Indeed, a fire destroyed several structures including two inns and a store on May 2, 1916, weakening the place economically. Then, in 1920, the city condemned the village as unsanitary since its sewage flowed directly into the ocean, and buildings were razed. Many of the Japanese families who called the village home moved to

Terminal Island near San Pedro, where they built another settlement and resumed fishing. But the Japanese presence in Santa Monica did not die with the fishing village. Some Japanese remained and other newcomers arrived. By the 1920s there were Japanese residents living in the canyon, in the mid-city area, and in Ocean Park, forming the seeds of what would become an active community.

The Jewish population, like other ethnic groups in the town, also had a distinctive role to play. Jews had long come to enjoy sylvan Santa Monica Canyon even before the town existed, and they were among the first to invest in land when town lots were auctioned in 1875. After this date, several prominent Jewish families from Los Angeles kept homes in Santa Monica, including Isaias Hellman, the well-respected president of the Farmers and Merchants Bank in Los Angeles. Other Jews settled in Santa Monica full time and began businesses. Norman Roth, a Jew from Illinois, came to the city in the 1880s and took over a general store that he ran with his brother Myron. Located on Third Street at Oregon (now Santa Monica Boulevard), the Roth Brothers promised groceries and dry goods that would "satisfy all in variety, quality and price." Later, in 1894, Roth was elected a city trustee and was popular enough to win reelection in 1898. Abraham Mooser was another merchant who helped supply Santa Monicans with their basic needs. The Bavarian-born Mooser came to the city with his wife and six children and took over a bankrupt store from one M.E. Chapin in 1891, turning it into a successful dry goods and clothing establishment. (In 1892 their seventh child, Carolyn, had the distinction of being the first Jewish person born in the city.) Like Roth, Mooser was very active in the city's civic and political life, helping to establish Woodlawn Cemetery among other activities.

Jews were also active participants in the city's early tourist trade. Mendel Meyer was famous "from San Francisco to Tombstone" as a Santa Monica Canyon entertainer (he played the violin) and storekeeper. In the city itself he was active in organizing events such as a well-attended ball held in 1879 at the Perkins House, one of Santa Monica's early hostelries. For devising this and other events, the *Los Angeles Evening Express* lauded Meyer's "untiring efforts to please the people of Santa Monica and visitors to the seaside." In the 1880s and 1890s Meyer also ran saloons in the city, including one on Third Street known as the Fireman and Turner's Retreat, which not only served eight different kinds of ice-cold beer and a "first class line of other liquors and cigars," but a free lunch to boot.[40] Jews also had a hand in the tourist hotels that increasingly attracted visitors to Santa Monica in its early years. Shortly after the grand Arcadia Hotel—a Santa Monica landmark at the time—was built in 1887, a Jewish lawyer from San Francisco named Henry Kowalski purchased it. Perhaps not coincidentally, the Arcadia was the preferred hostelry for Jewish visitors. Indeed, in subsequent years, the whole town of Santa Monica became a favored vacation spot for Jews from neighboring Los Angeles and farther afield and, by the 1890s, quite a few Jewish families were renting cottages in the city for the entire summer.

While Jews, African Americans, Asians, and others were present and busy making their mark on Santa Monica, there was one people most notable for their absence—the original inhabitants of the region, the Gabrielino Indians. It is in the period after the town was founded that they seem to disappear from the historical record in Santa Monica, an important, if tragic, moment for a people who had so long played a role in the area. Records of Indians in other parts of Southern California show that their fate continued to be bleak through the nineteenth and early twentieth centuries. As historian Carey McWilliams remarked, "In effect the Indians of California were ground to pieces between two invasions: the Spanish from the south up the coast and the Anglos from the east and north across the mountains and over the desert."[41] However, in the late 1800s there were still scattered Indian settlements in coastal Southern California. For example, Gabrielino people resided on the Palos Verdes peninsula throughout the nineteenth century. But overall, population movement (including to reservations), intermarriage with Hispanics, and absorption into the Hispanic population of the region meant their culture was ever more fragmented and their legacy less and less visible to the newcomers increasingly flooding the region.

Clearly Santa Monica has always had a diverse, multi-ethnic population and one can find evidence both of enmity and discrimination as well as cooperation and friendship among people of different backgrounds. In the years after the city's founding the Chinese bore the brunt of much hatred. Meanwhile, discrimination forced African Americans to develop separate institutions and get by with low-rung jobs and limited opportunities. Hispanics, for their part, were aware of the new dominance of white Americans and tensions sometimes arose between the two groups. In August of 1876, for example, a horsemanship contest was organized in Santa Monica pitting native Californian Juan J. Carrillo against a white American. The *Los Angeles Star* reported that "all of Los Angeles was there" to see whether the "pure American or the native Californian was the better knight." In a none too subtle account, the report continued that, "In the beginning of the tournament, the native Californian . . . seemed to have it all his own way, but American pluck and endurance will tell, and the result was that the American Eagle was once again triumphant."[42] This type of arrogance turned into more overt hostility once immigration from Mexico began to pick up in the 1910s. After World War I the anti-foreign feeling that swept America may have made groups such as the Japanese feel unwelcome.

On the other hand, Santa Monicans showed in other ways that they could learn to tolerate difference and ethnic groups could live comfortably together in the city's early decades. Jews, for example, were generally treated cordially in early Santa Monica, though elsewhere in the United States they faced considerable antagonism. And there was no bar to friendships such as that which arose between Celia Mooser, daughter of Jewish storekeeper Abraham Mooser, and Atala Carrillo, daughter of the Hispanic civic leader Juan Carrillo. Ethnic groups also mixed in places like the Canyon School, where black, white, Hispanic, Japanese, and Russian students learned and played together in the 1910s. And there were signs of slow progress, even in areas where discrimination prevailed. Donald Brunson, an early black resident, recalled that in the early 1920s he tried to join a white Boy Scout troop that met at the First Methodist Church. Though he was eventually allowed in, he acknowledged that, "We had trouble getting into it."[43] By 1925, however, a group of city realtors organized the city's first truly integrated troop, one of many small but significant steps toward greater equality.

Santa Monica was never a perfect paradise. Still, in its early days its residents were resourceful, energetic, and above all, busy making their new home livable. In some ways Santa Monica's early inhabitants were eager to replicate what they had known before coming to sunny Southern California. In its small mercantile emporiums, volunteer fire department, churches, and clubs, Santa Monica resembled Anytown, U.S.A. But despite these rather ordinary underpinnings, Santa Monica was special. Situated as it was on the edge of the Pacific, blessed by ideal weather, near the exploding metropolis of Los Angeles, in a region becoming glamorized by the nascent film industry, in a state that was attracting millions of eager new settlers, it had to be more than Anytown. So, as the city grew, its destiny as a capital of leisure and the good life unfolded as well.

Chapter Six

THE CITY FINDS A NICHE

As Santa Monica matured as a city and its people became settled over time, the city developed a distinctive identity—one that more than sustained it when dreams of railroads and ports came crashing down. Santa Monica was becoming first and foremost a resort city. In the early days the city did possess brick factories, a lumber yard, banks, and a small business district with stores to fulfill local needs. But between 1875 and 1930 neither manufacturing nor commerce drove the city. Likewise, early Santa Monica was home to agricultural enterprises where carnations, lima beans, and other produce were grown with great success. Its destiny, however, was not in farming. There was even a budding movie industry in the city in the early twentieth century. But Santa Monica's fame was not to be made as a movie capital. Instead, Santa Monica flourished as a leisure destination where the good life and activities like sea bathing, tennis, car racing, daring airplane flights, and even drinking were pursued with great interest. By the 1920s the revelry was in full swing, but two questions about what the city should be added a more serious note to these times. Residents struggled with the moral question of how much drinking, and the ills that accompanied it, should be tolerated in the city. Santa Monicans also wrestled with the political question of whether they should accept the tightening embrace of their neighbor Los Angeles or fight off her advances and remain an independent city. It was an interesting time indeed.

Santa Monica had been a leisure destination as early as the mid-nineteenth century, but as Southern California's population exploded in the late nineteenth and early twentieth centuries, Santa Monica grew to fill an important niche—helping former Easterners and Midwesterners live out the California dream. As newly-minted Angelinos flocked to Santa Monica for a taste of fun in the sun, so did some of the hundreds of thousands of tourists who streamed through the region, hungry for seaside amusement. It helped that the city was easily accessible. In the nineteenth century the Southern Pacific Railroad provided convenient service to Santa Monica. In 1889, for example, Southern Pacific trains were already bringing a whopping 200,000 people to Santa Monica a year, and as many as 12,000 in a single day; quite a large number for a city of only about 1,500 residents. This service was augmented when the Santa Fe Railroad built track to south Santa Monica (the Ocean Park area) in 1892 and ran up to seven trains a day to the new station. Using either railroad, it took only about thirty-five minutes to travel from downtown Los Angeles to Santa Monica. By 1896 Santa Monica was also served by electric streetcars from Los Angeles, operating as part of the Pasadena & Pacific line. Later these popular trolleys were absorbed into the Los Angeles Pacific Company and continued to operate from Los Angeles to Santa Monica and the Long Wharf. This line became part of the sprawling Pacific Electric system when ownership of Southern California's interurban electric trolleys was consolidated in 1911. Pacific Electric trains were often crowded and unpleasant to ride, but they did provide a reliable and relatively inexpensive way for people all along the Pacific Electric's 1,164 miles of track to reach Santa Monica. In a sense, the dream of Santa Monica as a railway depot never died—trains did come to the city, but their cargo wasn't coal or lumber, but hordes of pleasure-seekers.

After World War I, automobiles also brought increasing numbers of visitors to Santa Monica. Los Angeles fell in love with the car earlier than other cities. Tired of long commutes on increasingly decrepit streetcars, Angelinos bought cars at an astonishing rate and used them not only to commute to work, but also for leisurely "motoring" to destinations like Santa Monica. By 1920 Angelinos owned one car for every 3.6 residents, compared to one car per thirteen residents in the rest of the United States, and were clamoring for better roads on which to drive their new machines. In response, Los Angeles County upgraded and paved many roads in this era, including Wilshire Boulevard. By 1909 Wilshire was already an artery leading from downtown Los Angeles all the way to Santa Monica, with only a brief break at Westlake (now MacArthur) Park. Santa Monica city officials acknowledged this connection in 1914 by adopting the name Wilshire for the city's section of the road, replacing its former name—Nevada. The throngs that came and went from Santa Monica by car in the early twentieth century caused some of the city's first traffic jams. After one major event in Santa Monica in the 1910s, the *Los Angeles Times* reported:

> Automobiles lined up for miles and plodded their way back to Los Angeles. There was no use endeavoring to speed. There were too many machines. From the summit of one hill between Santa Monica and the city the long line of automobiles . . . resembled a mammoth serpent crawling over the roads.[44]

Whether people came by public transportation or by private automobile, Santa Monica offered diverse attractions once they arrived. Initially, of course, it was the rustic atmosphere of Santa Monica Canyon that brought visitors. Once the town of Santa Monica was founded in 1875, enterprising individuals quickly began to capitalize on the town's lovely seaside location, mountainous backdrop, and fine weather. It was North Beach (north of today's Colorado Avenue), near where many of the town's first houses and businesses were located, that was first developed for tourists. Indeed, in 1876, only about a year after the town's first lots were auctioned off, a bathhouse was constructed there by Michael Duffy just north of the Los Angeles & Independence Railroad's pier. A hotel, aptly named the Santa Monica Hotel, also opened its doors in the first year of the town's existence. And Senator Jones, still in the first blush of optimism about his new town's prospects, played a role in building the Santa Monica Bathhouse, which opened in 1877 complete with steam baths and a plunge. One tourist to Santa Monica in 1877, Jennie Collier, recorded her impressions of the area's attractions:

> Santa Monica has a beach, a dock and a hotel and is therefore a popular
> summer resort for the people of the neighboring cities and foothills.
> If you choose to live like an English gentleman you can have a cottage
> down there to which you can take your whole family including the cat,
> dog, mockingbird, baby and Chinaman and revel in the soft breeze
> without being deprived of a single domestic joy. Or if the swelling in
> your pocketbook is only intermittent . . . you may take a room at the
> hotel, soak yourself in the surf in the morning, ride on the beach in
> the afternoon and flirt inanely in the evening. . . . Here you find an
> extensive bath house where you can soak yourself in the oceanic fluid,
> hot, cold, fresh, salt. . . . But before preparing for the drenching it is
> customary to throw yourself with studied carelessness upon the beach
> and twirl the warm sparkling sand through your fingers . . . [45]

While this experience was clearly delightful, it was soon curtailed when crisis hit the town in the late 1870s. Senator Jones's railroad, on which the hopes of the fledgling city were pinned, failed, and residents and businesses fled the town. The Santa Monica Hotel closed and, for a time, Santa Monica's future as a tourist spot looked dim. Slowly, however, the town revived, in part because visitors continued to come. The 1880s were boom years for most of Southern California, and newcomers from the East and Midwest wanted to enjoy the beach. The Santa Monica Hotel reopened in 1882 and it even added a score of additional rooms the following year. By the summer of 1887 some 2,000 to 3,000 people a day were flocking to North Beach to enjoy its leisure offerings. The beach became even more attractive in 1894 when the North Beach Bathhouse opened, advertising "hot and salt water baths every day of the year," as well as amenities such as a drawing room, ballroom, rooftop garden, two dining rooms, and a bowling pavilion.[46] Not long afterwards, the Camera Obscura was built at North Beach by Robert F. Jones to further delight visitors. This unusual structure, which was later moved and now stands in Palisades Park, was a forerunner to the modern camera. The building featured a revolving turret with a mirror that reflected exterior images down through a convex lens onto a table inside.

The Arcadia Hotel, built in 1887, was the jewel in the crown of Santa Monica's thriving beach scene. Named for Arcadia Bandini de Baker, an important force in Santa Monica's early development, it too offered a bathhouse, but much more besides. Located on the edge of the bluff just south of today's Colorado Avenue, the Arcadia was a massive, five-story, 150-room establishment that boasted an airy ballroom with a "first-class" orchestra, a huge dining room, parlor, billiard and reading rooms, well-tended flower gardens, and a cupola affording panoramic views of the coast. Like other highbrow tourist hotels built around the same time, such as the Hotel del Coronado near San Diego, the Arcadia was an institution that offered clients a sort of East Coast refinement where, for example, lectures on Shakespeare might be offered in what was otherwise an unpolished town. Given these amenities, combined with those offered at North Beach, it was with some justification that boosters billed Santa Monica as "the leading coast resort of the Pacific" by the 1890s.[47]

But fashions change and even as the northern part of the city enjoyed its heyday as a tourist destination, the southern part of Santa Monica, what came to be called Ocean Park, was on the rise. In the 1870s the first white Americans had settled there on land that had been part of old Rancho La Ballona. The new owners, Mrs. Lucas and her sons, then commenced farming their 861-acre parcel. In 1884, as real estate was booming in Southern California, W.D. Vawter and his son E.J. purchased one hundred of these acres and began to subdivide them into residential parcels. In 1892 Abbot Kinney, the Renaissance man and real estate promoter who would also develop adjacent Venice, bought an oceanfront strip of the Vawter holdings in partnership with Francis C. Ryan. Their firm, the Ocean Park Development Company, would give the area not only its name but also its flavor as a vibrant tourist destination.

By the late 1890s, Santa Monica's southside was developing into a community in its own right. As the *Outlook* reported in 1899:

> there are now 200 cottages on this property, a great many of which were erected last year. . . . These cottages are not mere shacks, but they will be neat and commodious, costing all the way from $350 to $1000. They are being put up by first-class tenants, mostly professional and business men from Los Angeles.[48]

Before long Ocean Park also had a bank, post office, church, and small businesses, and was integrated into regional transportation networks both by train (the Santa Fe began serving Ocean Park in 1892) and electric streetcar. Local travelers could also use a horse-drawn trolley that ferried between north and south Santa Monica, or simply stroll the boardwalks linking the two areas. By 1902 there were 700 cottages and the area continued to grow at a striking pace.

Ocean Park's reputation as a leisure destination blossomed as well. In its earliest years it was home to some quirky attractions. An ostrich farm was started there in 1889 by an Englishman with experience raising these birds and attracting visitors to see them. This enterprise ceased operation in 1895, but not before residents witnessed the escape of one large African ostrich, which ran all the way to the Sawtelle area, frantically dashed back, and then overshot the farm to meet its death in the Pacific. Another early attraction was E.J. Vawter's carnation farm on Fourth Street. Started in 1899, it was well known for its magnificent fields of carnations, roses, and other blooms. A YMCA camp located on five acres of beachfront property near Hill Street also attracted visitors for lectures, concerts, and overnight stays. The first hotel built on the southside had less success. After its opening in 1898 it welcomed visitors for only a few days before burning down.

It was the piers of Ocean Park (and nearby Venice) that really brought in the crowds and propelled the area to prominence as a superb place for tourists and day-trippers from Los Angeles. Abbot Kinney, on the lookout for ways to enhance the value of his real estate ventures, was instrumental in building a couple of them. Ocean Park's first pier was constructed by the Santa Fe Railroad in 1895 in exchange for land Kinney donated for a Santa Fe depot. At only a few hundred feet long, this "pleasure pier" was something of a flop. Kinney himself built a second pier around 1900, which was longer and succeeded in attracting fishermen but not many tourists. Then, in 1904, he turned his energy to developing Venice of America and built the very popular Venice Pier. Meanwhile, a series of other piers were built in Ocean Park with varying success, including the Horseshoe Pier and Pavilion at Marine Street just north of the Venice border; and the Crystal Pier at the end of Hollister Avenue, which featured Nat Goodwin's Café, frequented by early movie stars including Charlie Chaplin. The huge and successful Million Dollar Pier, opened in 1911, replaced the old Horseshoe Pier and boasted an amusement park, dance hall, carousels, restaurants, and other attractions, but was destroyed by fire only two years later. Pier builders abhorred a vacuum, however, and three side-by-side piers rose from the water at the same location—the Pickering Pleasure Pier, the G.M. Jones Pier, and the Dome Pier.

The early twentieth century was the heyday of Ocean Park. Besides its exciting piers, it lured pleasure-seekers to "the Coney Island of the Pacific" with numerous dance halls, casinos, plunges, auditoriums, theatres, saloons, roller-coasters, and plentiful opportunities for people-watching. Indeed, by World War I it had far eclipsed Santa Monica's North Beach as the place to go in the city. Around 1915 a guidebook to Southern California described Ocean Park and its neighbor Venice:

> These places are full of hotels and lodging-houses, mostly of the less pretentious and inexpensive class, and they are filled during the winter season mainly by Eastern tourists. In the summer the immense bathing beaches attract crowds from the city. The Pacific Electric brings its daily contingent of tourists and the streets are constantly crowded with motors—sometimes hundreds of them. All of which contribute to the animation of the scene in these popular resorts.

The north side of Santa Monica, once so attractive to tourists, was described as having "a different atmosphere; it is a residence town with no 'amusement' features and few hotels, depending on its neighbors for these useful adjuncts."[49] The once regal Arcadia had long since disappeared, having been converted into a military academy and then torn down in 1908. Although a North Beach Bathhouse Pier had been constructed in 1898 it was short and the most exciting things that happened there were fishing and walking. The Municipal Pier, built in 1909 at the foot of Colorado Avenue and still standing today, was also less than thrilling. It functioned well as a conduit for the city's sewage to be pumped out into the bay, served fishermen, and allowed nice views from its sea end, but it wasn't enough to bring in great crowds. By World War I the North Beach area was definitely in the doldrums. Even city officials acknowledged that Santa Monica (by that they meant north Santa Monica) was a "dead town."[50]

But tourists are fickle, always on the lookout for the newest thing, and before long the northside would be jumping again. And, as immigration to the Southland picked up and reached a crescendo in the 1920s, there were plenty of newcomers eager to share in the delights offered by both the north and south sides of the city. While Venice and Ocean Park would continue to specialize in amusements for ordinary folks and revel in a honky-tonk atmosphere, the northside aimed for a different market, providing fun for the "highest class of people."[51] By the 1920s the more northern area of Santa Monica emerged as a world-renowned resort for the rich and famous with fancy beach clubs, exclusive homes, and an economy dedicated to the pursuit of pleasure.

The Santa Monica Pleasure Pier, also known as the Looff Pier, kicked off this trend. Masterminded by veteran amusement operator Charles Looff, the massive pier was directly adjacent to the city's Municipal Pier. Opened in 1916, it included the "Blue Streak Racer" rollercoaster, a funhouse, billiards and bowling facilities, carnival rides, a bandstand where live music was played every day, a picnic area, a restaurant and banquet hall, and the carousel building that still stands today on the Santa Monica Pier. (Today's Santa Monica Pier is a combination of the 1909 Municipal Pier and the Looff Pier.) Conceived as a "Refined Amusement Center" where no alcohol was served, the pier succeeded in once again attracting throngs of beachgoers to north Santa Monica.

Its popularity surged even higher when a new roller-coaster, The Whirlwind Dipper, and the largest ballroom on the West Coast, the legendary La Monica, opened on the pier in 1924. Coincidentally, 1924 was also the year a devastating fire ravaged much of Ocean Park's amusement zone and piers, sending extra business to the Pleasure Pier. Located at the far end of the pier, the La Monica Ballroom was a fantasy of Spanish-style architecture by way of the Middle East, accented with numerous minarets that glowed by night. The interior was done up in "modified French Renaissance" style and could accommodate up to 5,000 guests at a time. From the beginning the La Monica was something special. Its gala opening in the summer of 1924 was attended by some of Hollywood's most famous silent-film stars, who arrived by limousine. Some 25,000 ordinary people showed up to mark the event and take a turn on the 15,000-square-foot maple dance floor. Through the 1920s the La Monica hosted well-known bands, Charleston dance contests, college nights, and celebrity appearances.

Exclusive beach clubs, clustered on the mile-and-a-half strip of beach extending north from Pico Boulevard, also flourished in 1920s Santa Monica and contributed to the city's lively scene. Beach clubs were a fad of the 1920s and the Los Angeles coastline had more than 200 such institutions in 1927, expressing the hedonistic spirit of the time. In Santa Monica the Santa Monica Athletic Club, the Beach Club, the Santa Monica Swimming Club, the Deauville, the Wavecrest, the Gables, the Edgewater, and the Breakers clubs, to name a few, were all founded in the 1920s and maintained impressive clubhouses that appealed to different factions of the area's upper crust. The Santa Monica Swimming Club, for example, was known for its Hollywood crowd membership and for its swinging parties, with one former member describing the atmosphere there as "gay and dressy." The largest of the clubs was Club Casa del Mar, which had 5,000 members at its peak and

Continued on p. 95

Native Peoples of California drawn by A.L. Kroeber. (From R.F. Heizer and A.B. Elsasser, The Natural World of the California Indians. *Berkeley: University of California Press, 1980.)*

View of the palisades and mouth of Santa Monica Canyon c. 1870. (Courtesy of the Santa Monica Public Library Image Archives, Security First National Bank Collection.)

*Native Americans building San Gabriel Mission under Spanish supervision. Throughout the colonial period Indians far outnumbered Spanish settlers in the Los Angeles area and provided most of the labor for Spanish projects. (*San Gabriel Mission and the Beginnings of Los Angeles, *Alexander Harmer.)*

San Gabriel Mission, c. 1900. (Author's collection.)

San Gabriel Mission, So. California.

*A Native American drives a carreta. In the nineteenth century every rancho used these primitive vehicles to haul hides, grapes, and other products, as well as to transport women and children. (*San Gabriel Mission and the Beginnings of Los Angeles, *Arthur B. Dodge.)*

This photograph of three nattily dressed Californios, members of the Sepúlveda and Yorba families, was taken around 1858 when Hispanic ranching families controlled all of the Santa Monica area. (Courtesy of the Santa Monica Public Library Image Archives, Title Insurance and Trust Collection.)

Santa Monica's popularity as a tourist spot began with camping. This 1878 image shows families posing near their canvas tents where some were probably spending the entire summer. (Courtesy of the Santa Monica Public Library Image Archives, Security First National Bank Collection.)

Senator John P. Jones of Nevada. Jones founded the town of Santa Monica and promoted it as a railroad terminus and regional port in the 1870s. (Courtesy Library of Congress.)

*Santa Monica's founder, John P. Jones, represented the state of Nevada as a United States senator for three decades, but still managed to spend time at his "Miramar" home on Ocean Avenue. The lavish house befitted his status as a silver tycoon. Today the Miramar Hotel stands on the site of Jones's home. (*Santa Monica Blue Book.*)*

*Railroad magnate Collis Huntington hoped to monopolize railroad traffic in the Los Angeles area and make Santa Monica a shipping center by building Port Los Angeles, also known as the Long Wharf. This 1892 view shows the wharf before its official opening. (*Santa Monica Community Book.*)*

*Arcadia Bandini de Baker, the daughter of prominent Californio Juan Bandini, was a major landowner in the Santa Monica area, a generous donor to many civic projects, and the wife of Colonel Robert S. Baker. (*Santa Monica Community Book.*)*

This view of the palisades, taken around 1910, shows the railroad tracks leading to the Long Wharf and the wharf itself in the far distance. No longer used for freight trains by this time, an electric passenger trolley can be seen on the tracks. (Author's collection.)

The congregation of the Colored Methodist Episcopal Church (now the Christian Methodist Episcopal Church) in 1910. Discouraged from worshipping with whites, Santa Monica's oldest African-American church built a permanent home in the Phillips Chapel at Fourth and Bay Streets. (Courtesy of the Santa Monica Public Library Image Archives, Donald Brunson, Sr. Collection.)

*View of Third Street, the city's main business and shopping center, looking north from Broadway in 1891. (*Santa Monica Blue Book.*)*

*This 1898 view of the North Beach area shows the dwellings of summer campers on the sand, the "99 steps" leading down from the bluffs, and the outline of the Arcadia Hotel in the far distance past the pier. (*Santa Monica Blue Book.*)*

*Opened in 1894, the North Beach Bathhouse offered amenities including a ballroom, bowling pavilion, and rooftop garden, as well as "hot and salt water baths every day of the year." Photograph c. 1900. (*Santa Monica Blue Book.*)*

Ocean Park was mostly undeveloped when this photograph was taken around 1895. The pier pictured was Ocean Park's first. (Courtesy Research Library, The Getty Research Institute, Los Angeles 830032.)

*The north side of Santa Monica was a tourist mecca in the late nineteenth century. This image, taken around 1900, shows crowds in front of the North Beach Bathhouse (with arches at far left) and the pointed cupola of the Arcadia Hotel rising behind it. (*Santa Monica Blue Book.*)*

Postcards like this one put out by the Southern Pacific Railroad helped attract newcomers to Southern California in the late nineteenth and early twentieth centuries. (Author's collection.)

*From its founding Santa Monica was easily accessible from Los Angeles by train, increasing its popularity as a seaside resort. Here electric streetcars arrive in Santa Monica in April of 1896. (*Santa Monica Blue Book.*)*

Palisades Park around the turn of the twentieth century. Established early in the city's history, the park makes Santa Monica one of the few municipalities in California that have preserved ocean views for public enjoyment. (Author's collection.)

Santa Monica beachgoers took a moment to show off their swim togs for photographer H.F. Rile in 1910. (Santa Monica Blue Book.)

This view of Franklin Hill (looking north from near today's Montana Avenue and Twenty-fourth Street) suggests how sparsely settled some parts of the city were even in the 1920s. (Courtesy Franklin Elementary School.)

Southern California was world famous for its orange groves, but Santa Monica's seaside climate was better suited to lima beans. This warehouse near Eighteenth Street and Colorado Avenue, photographed c. 1916, stored the local crop. (Courtesy Franklin Elementary School.)

The promise of a tidy bungalow under sunny skies drew Americans from the East and Midwest to Santa Monica in the 1920s. This postcard was sent to France in 1923. The sender pointed out that these houses were the "homes of ordinary workers," emphasizing that the good life here was open to all. (Author's collection.)

Los Angeles c. 1905 was already a congested, highly urban place as seen in this view of Spring Street. No wonder Angelinos enjoyed getting away for a day at the beach in Santa Monica. (Author's collection.)

Racers crank up their engines for the 1916 Vanderbilt Cup race that transformed Santa Monica's streets into a speedway. Palisades Park is in the background. Note the special streetcar that helped bring thousands to the city on race day. (Courtesy of Phil Harms.)

This view of Ocean Avenue near Idaho shows the 1914 Vanderbilt Cup race in progress with #12 Ralph DePalma in his Mercedes on the way to victory. Wooden bridges were built over the racecourse to keep spectators out of the way of speeding cars. (Courtesy of Phil Harms.)

By 1927 automobiles were already creating congestion on Third Street at Broadway in the city's bustling business district. (Courtesy of the Santa Monica Public Library Image Archives, Adelbert Bartlett photographer.)

View looking north from around Strand Street to the Looff Pier, c. 1927. Santa Monica's beaches were jam-packed with fun-seekers through the 1920s. (Courtesy of the Santa Monica Public Library Image Archives, Adelbert Bartlett photographer.)

Santa Monica's women excelled at tennis in the early twentieth century, winning many national and international titles. Here Clara Bartlett shows off her form at Lincoln Park (now Reed Park) c. 1925. (Courtesy of the Santa Monica Public Library Image Archives, Adelbert Bartlett photographer.)

Nestled under the palisades north of the pier, the "Gold Coast" colony was home to numerous movie stars beginning in the 1920s. This image dates from around the late 1930s. (Santa Monica Blue Book.)

Even the Depression could not stop these Children's Day Parade participants from enjoying themselves c. 1930. (Courtesy of the Santa Monica Public Library Image Archives, Adelbert Bartlett photographer.)

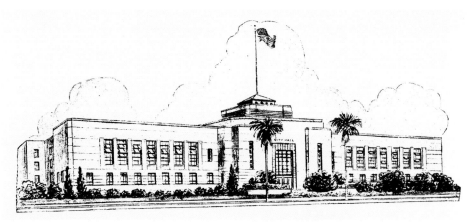

City hall, built in 1938–1939, was one of several major public works projects funded by the federal government during the Depression in Santa Monica. (Santa Monica Blue Book.)

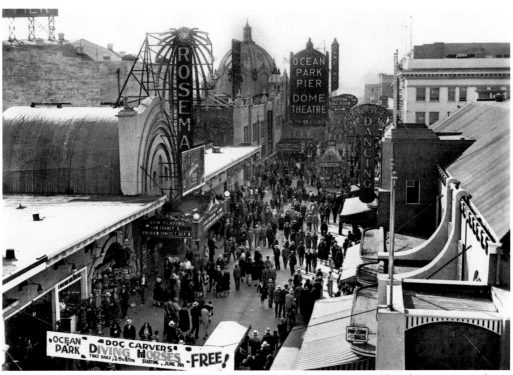

The Ocean Park Pier as it appeared c. 1930. (Courtesy of the Santa Monica Public Library Image Archives, Adelbert Bartlett photographer.)

Local bathing beauties posed for a photo to celebrate the opening of a new bus turntable in Ocean Park, May 1934. Note the African-American boy at the back of the bus. (Courtesy of Big Blue Bus.)

This 1935 view of the city's newly opened yacht harbor looked promising, but the harbor was expensive to maintain and never very popular with boaters. The Deauville Club is visible in the top right of the picture. (Courtesy of the Santa Monica Public Library Image Archives, Adelbert Bartlett photographer.)

Bay Cities Guaranty Building and Loan Association built the city's first high rise in 1929 at 221–223 Santa Monica Boulevard. The Outlook *declared the building "a step forward in the advancement of the business section of Santa Monica and a vast change in Santa Monica's skyline." (*Santa Monica Blue Book.*)*

Route 66—America's favorite highway—followed Santa Monica Boulevard to its end point at Palisades Park. For decades the fabled road brought newcomers to the city looking for a piece of the California dream. (Courtesy of the Santa Monica Public Library Image Archives, Adelbert Bartlett photographer.)

During the Depression the city built a new breakwater and harbor. This aerial view of the coast, c. 1940, shows a portion of the breakwater (upper right corner), anchored boats, and the huge buildup of sand on the north side of the pier the project caused. The large structure on the pier is the La Monica Ballroom. (Courtesy of the Santa Monica Public Library Image Archives, Randy Young Collection.)

Starting in the 1930s, well-honed bodies and amazing stunts made Santa Monica's Muscle Beach world famous. In this photo Harold Zinkin (in backbend) supports (from bottom) Moe Most, Jack LaLanne, and Gene Miller. (Courtesy of Harold Zinkin.)

*Aviation great Donald W. Douglas, c. 1940. (*Santa Monica Blue Book.*)*

To produce all the planes needed during World War II, thousands of women were hired at Douglas Aircraft in Santa Monica. But more workers were always needed. Here Douglas employees demonstrate tool use for a group of potential hires on "Opportunity Day." (Courtesy of the Santa Monica Public Library Image Archives, Museum of Flying Collection.)

A lone worker walks under the camouflage concealing Douglas Aircraft from view during World War II. The burlap camouflage was made to look like a residential neighborhood from the air and covered the entire factory. A "dummy plant" was even built nearby to further protect the factory from air attacks. (Courtesy of the Santa Monica Public Library Image Archives, Museum of Flying Collection.)

Housing shortages were a major problem during World War II as thousands of military personnel and civilians flooded into Santa Monica for the duration. This trailer park near the palisades housed Douglas Aircraft employees. (Courtesy of the Santa Monica Public Library Image Archives, Museum of Flying Collection.)

In the mid-twentieth century, city officials worked to destroy hundreds of poor-quality dwellings. In 1953 the city's sanitation inspector supervised the burning of this house on Belmar Place between Main and Third, where the Civic Center is now located. Ironically, in 1999 the city made a similar "Shotgun House" a historic landmark. (Courtesy of the Santa Monica Public Library Image Archives.)

In an effort to revive downtown shopping the city built pedestrian-friendly Santa Monica Mall on Third Street between Wilshire and Broadway. This 1965 photo shows the Mall under construction. The street was redesigned again in the 1980s as the Third Street Promenade. (Courtesy of the Santa Monica Public Library Image Archives.)

Continued from p. 66

was housed in a lavishly decorated building located near Ocean and Pico (the building still stands today as the Hotel Casa del Mar). Casa del Mar was the favored meeting place for business and professional people who mixed at dances in its ballroom, in its Olympic-size pool, at meals in its posh dining room, and at athletic competitions, concerts, and barbecues on the sand. Club Casa del Mar and the other beach clubs offered non-stop fun for their high-rolling clientele who found Santa Monica the best place to see and be seen.

Attractions like the La Monica Ballroom were rather democratic, open to those who could afford a night out. The city's beach clubs were far more exclusive, welcoming mostly the well-to-do or famous. Of an even more exalted status was Santa Monica's "Gold Coast" enclave of Hollywood film stars that settled in the city in the 1920s. In the movie industry's earliest years, film actors and actresses lived relatively normal lives. Soon enough, however, the star system took hold and successful players were increasingly well-paid. Hollywood's royalty wanted real estate to match their wealth and fame and set about creating lavish estates such as Mary Pickford and Douglas Fairbanks's Pickfair. And starting in the 1920s—just as many of today's film stars maintain homes in Malibu—some of Hollywood's biggest celebrities built homes in Santa Monica, flocking together in a colony built along the narrow coast road (today's Pacific Coast Highway) under Palisades Park. Pickford and Fairbanks built a "cottage" there that was small only when compared to Pickfair. The great comic actor Harold Lloyd, his frequent co-star Bebe Daniels, diva Norma Shearer, as well as actors Richard Barthelmess, Owen Moore, Edmund Goulding, and Jack Doyle joined them. Mack Sennett, Louis B. Mayer, and Jesse Lasky, all luminaries of the motion-picture industry, built elegant and expensive beach homes too. The most palatial of all was actress Marion Davies's estate, part of which still stands at 415 Pacific Coast Highway. Built for her in 1928 by her mentor and companion, newspaper magnate William Randolph Hearst, the Davies property had over one hundred rooms, some imported in their entirety from castles in Europe. Ceilings done up in gold leaf, rare antiques throughout, tennis courts, and a vast swimming pool lined in Italian marble added to the scene, dubbed "Hollywood's Versailles" by one writer, where some of the era's most legendary parties were held.[52] Symbolic of the excesses of both Hollywood and the 1920s, these houses and their glamorous inhabitants galvanized the city's reputation as a glittering destination where enjoying life was a top priority.

All across the social spectrum Santa Monica offered opportunities for the enjoyment of leisure activities, and not all were confined to the beach. Santa Monicans were devoted to sports of all kinds and the city produced many champion athletes in these years. The city's sporty tone was set early on. One of the first organizations to be founded in Santa Monica was a baseball club, in the same year the town was founded. As early as 1880 Santa Monicans were already staging polo matches in what is now Christine Emerson Reed Park, and the city was one of the first communities in California with its own polo pitch. Santa Monicans were also in the vanguard when it came to cricket and cycling. Moreover, Santa Monica's founders, Senator John P. Jones and Colonel Robert Baker, joined with other notables in the area such as Abbot Kinney to form the Santa Monica Improvement Club in 1887. Despite its name, tennis was its preoccupation and the club encouraged the sport by building a clubhouse and courts on Third Street near Washington, and by hosting annual regional tournaments beginning in 1887. Later, under the guidance of tennis-enthusiast and mayor, T.H. Dudley, the city built public courts (also at today's Reed Park), which served as the training ground for numerous champions in the early twentieth century.

Indeed, to say that Santa Monicans excelled in tennis early on is a vast understatement. As *Outlook* editor and historian Charles Warren remarked, "So many times has Santa Monica won a place in the tennis sun, a larger place than any other city can claim, that it is difficult indeed for any historian to express its true measure in mere tournament records."[53] However, mentioning a few does give an idea of the pinnacle of excellence achieved in Santa Monica, particularly among women. To begin with, Marion Jones, the daughter of Senator Jones, was a national champion in 1899 and again in 1902. Mary Browne won the national championship three times in 1912, 1913, and 1914, as well as the national doubles championship five times. May Sutton also won the national championship, but then went on to international acclaim by winning Wimbledon in 1905 and 1907. Elizabeth "Bunny" Ryan was an astonishing eighteen-time winner at Wimbledon, with victories spanning from 1914 until 1934 playing doubles and mixed doubles. In 1926 Johnnie Doeg was a local champion but later went on to win national titles twice, vanquishing his opponents with his powerful "cannonball" service. The name Santa Monica was known far and wide thanks to the feats of these prodigious athletes, and more stars came out of Santa Monica in the 1930s and 1940s to carry on the tradition of tennis excellence they began.

In the 1920s Santa Monicans also pursued sports that would come to symbolize the California lifestyle. Sam Reid and Tom Blake were lifeguards at the Santa Monica Swimming Club, located just south of Santa Monica Canyon. They were also pioneer surfers who not only practiced the sport when few others did but also tested new surfboard designs. Blake was also an innovator in board design and was important enough to the sport to be included recently in the Surfing Walk of Fame in Huntington Beach. In the 1920s volleyball was relatively new and Santa Monica's beach clubs, where volleyball grew to be immensely popular, played a role in expanding interest in the game.

Certainly many other Southern California communities shared in this passion for sports. As one early twentieth-century observer of the region remarked, "The climate is so entirely congenial to the American athletics mania that sports flourish and 'champions' are a major product." The tendency of Californians to be sporty was even confirmed in scientific studies conducted around this time, which concluded that California college girls, for example, were not only larger than their East Coast counterparts, but also had "larger biceps and calves, and a superiority of tested strength."[54] But Santa Monicans went beyond this already high norm of interest and achievement in sports and would continue to innovate in athletics for decades to come.

The City Finds a Niche

Thrilling automobile races, held in the city from 1909 until 1919, offered another chance for residents and thousands of visitors to enjoy themselves and also helped spread the city's fame. Road races, conducted on ordinary roads or streets rather than on a racetrack, began when the auto industry was in its infancy. Eager to test the abilities of their models and gain publicity for successful cars, early manufacturers and auto dealers encouraged racing in many communities and enthusiastic drivers obliged. Cities like Santa Monica were eager to join the trend, seeing road racing as a means of advertising themselves and, with luck, attracting new residents. The first Santa Monica road race in 1909 was organized by the Automobile Dealers Association of Southern California, but city officials lent their support by volunteering to build grandstands and other amenities while the *Outlook* encouraged residents to assist in any way they could. They did their work well and the 1909 race was a great success. Apparently the chance to see the West Coast's first major automobile race was a powerful draw, because thousands showed up to watch stripped-down stock cars circle a course that began on Ocean Avenue, went up Nevada (now Wilshire) to the corner of today's Veterans Administration complex, then back down San Vicente to Ocean, with grandstands and the start/finish line on Ocean.

Hopes were high for another exciting race with a high turnout in 1910. A motion picture was to be made of the race and the *Outlook* hoped that "showing Santa Monica bay on a balmy winter day, kissed by the sun's rays with automobiles dashing through beautiful palms and roses was sure to bring good results."[55] Certainly the race attracted people from all over Los Angeles. Excitement ran so high that by midnight on the night before the race, 10,000 enthusiastic people were already within a mile of the grandstand. *Motor Age* reported that:

> After dancing on an immense platform for several hours the fog and the chill morning air proved too much for the awaiting spectators and they proceeded to demolish said dance hall and burn it up in several gigantic bonfires. The special police who dared to interfere were threatened with a ducking in the ocean and retired. The beach resorts for miles along the coast were crowded throughout the night and those who could not find better accommodations slept in the sand and under the many palm trees.[56]

By 1911 the Santa Monica Road Races were starting to garner more national publicity, as well as some national teams who arrived with their autos by rail with spare parts and mechanics in tow. Again, spectators turned out en masse. A *Los Angeles Times* reporter's description of what is now Wilshire Boulevard is richly evocative of the scene on race morning:

A trip down Nevada avenue displayed numerous little bonfires where coffee was being heated and bacon and eggs fried, and by the side of the lowly camp stood a magnificent $5000 automobile which had been the sleeping place for the owners and their friends.[57]

Santa Monica

Lucky spectators would soon be seeing driver Harvey Herrick setting a world record for a 200-mile road race—an amazing (for the time) 74.603 miles per hour. Meanwhile, Santa Monicans rented out their spare rooms to visitors and some with homes on the race course built bleachers and hosted race parties for their friends.

Each year brought greater crowds, better-known drivers, more specialized cars, and more publicity for the city. By 1912 Barney Oldfield, who race historians Harold Osmer and Phil Harms call "the most famous driver of them all," came and new speed records were set. In 1913 an estimated 40,000 to 50,000 people attended, and that was considered a low year. By 1914 the Santa Monica Road Races were in the big time, drawing top-ranked racers not only from the United States, but also France, Italy, Germany, and England. This was the first year two major separate races were run in Santa Monica—the Vanderbilt Cup and the American Grand Prize. The city was overrun by an estimated 100,000 spectators from far and wide who came to witness these spectacles that combined human daring with automotive power. They were not disappointed when both races produced new speed records. Reporters from across the nation were there too and they spread the word that Santa Monica was indeed a very exciting place to be.

No races were held in Santa Monica in 1915, but in 1916 both the Vanderbilt Cup and the Grand Prize returned to the city. Again world records for speed were set and the crowds were larger than ever, though tragically five people, including several bystanders, were killed as a car careened off the roadway. This accident, along with the coming of World War I, halted the races for two years and dampened local enthusiasm for automobile contests in the city. Indeed, by 1919, when the last road races were held in Santa Monica, the city no longer needed the publicity these events offered—tourists and new residents were coming for a whole host of other attractions—and road racing was increasingly dangerous.

For one thing, Santa Monica had seen much development since 1909 and cars no longer raced through mostly empty fields, but instead past homes and well-tended gardens. As automotive technology developed, the cars themselves were becoming too fast to race on ordinary streets. Still, a host of professional drivers arrived for one last race and organizers pronounced it too a success. The 1919 race marked the end of an era—not only for road racing, but for Santa Monica as a capitol of automotive competition. However, leisure and excitement were far from dead in the city. The very person who served as honorary referee for the 1919 races—screen idol Douglas Fairbanks—as well as the many other Hollywood stars who attended that year, were a link to the fun-loving, glamorous Santa Monica of the 1920s.

The tradition of performing daring feats in newly-invented machines was also carried forward into 1920s Santa Monica, with airplanes taking the place of racecars. In fact Santa Monica was home to one of the era's most extraordinary aviation achievements—the first around-the-world airplane flight in 1924. It was a young Donald Douglas who made it happen. Douglas, like many aviation pioneers, was drawn to the Southland in the early twentieth century and, by the early 1920s, founded Douglas Aircraft Company. Passing a spacious former movie studio located in Santa Monica's unpopulated northeastern end one day (where Douglas Park is today), Douglas decided to set up shop and was soon making innovative planes for the Navy there. Not long afterwards, he was approached about producing four aircraft for a possible around-the-world flight manned by U.S. Army pilots. A technical genius as well as a talented entrepreneur, Douglas jumped at the chance and in early 1924 four brand-new Douglas World Cruisers were wheeled from Douglas's Wilshire Boulevard plant to the take-off site at Clover Field. (At some residential parts of the route, trees had to be trimmed and mailboxes removed to allow these new-fangled machines by.)

The four Army pilots took off on March 17, 1924, and did not land again at Santa Monica until September 23. But during their 160 days away, the men succeeded in traversing over 28,000 miles to become the first to successfully circle the earth by air. Naturally there was a vast crowd on hand to welcome them on their return. As the *Outlook* reported that day in a special edition:

> the storm-battered planes of the Around-the-World Aviators landed here today. A colorful crowd, estimated at 50,000, has gathered to welcome the first aviators to circumnavigate the globe. The planes . . . settled to earth here amidst the deafening shouts of welcome of Southern California. It marked the end of the greatest epoch of the aerial age and started a new period in man's mastery over the elements.[58]

Donald Douglas and his planes would have a long-term effect on the city, but at this moment Santa Monicans simply went wild with the thrilling news and Santa Monica was again publicized around the world, thrust into the spotlight as a place where extraordinary people did exciting things.

Men were not the only ones drawn to Santa Monica to make a mark on aviation history; women too were attracted to the excitement of flying. In 1929, twenty of the world's most accomplished female pilots, including Amelia Earhart, gathered at Santa Monica's Clover Field for the start of the first women's cross-country air race. From its beginning there, the race covered 2,700 miles to terminate in Cleveland, Ohio nine days later. Dubbed the Powder Puff Derby by humorist Will Rogers, the race was an opportunity for the female pilots to show off their skills and demonstrate that women could fly planes as well as men. As with the Around-the-World Flight in 1924, the contest held the nation's attention, brought fame to the daring pilots, and reinforced Santa Monica's reputation as a center for thrilling innovation in flight.

The pursuit of pleasure and excitement was a central focus of life in Santa Monica from the town's earliest days when the first bathhouses opened, all the way through the 1920s. Yet in some ways, the town was deeply conflicted about its identity, especially when the fun involved alcohol. Indeed, just as rent control has been a persistent and divisive issue in Santa Monica in the last several decades, the fight over temperance was a long-running point of contention for early Santa Monicans. The debate was propelled by two factors. First, the nation as a whole was increasingly viewing alcohol as a problem in the late nineteenth and early twentieth centuries, a concern that would culminate in the 1919 Volstead Act ordering nationwide prohibition of alcohol. Second, as a center of leisure, there was simply a lot of drinking going on in Santa Monica, making residents particularly aware of the problem and eager to solve it.

Even nineteenth-century Santa Monica was something of a magnet for drinkers, with many saloons lining Utah (now Broadway) as well as drinking establishments near the beach. One of the main functions of the police in that era was, in fact, the management of the many inebriated men who staggered out of these establishments. When the Long Wharf was operating in the 1890s, watering holes in Santa Monica Canyon did a brisk business serving dockworkers, sailors, and others passing through. By the turn of the century, as the population of the city and neighboring Los Angeles grew, consumption of alcohol seems to have grown as well. Historians Marvin Wolf and Katharine Madar have noted that, by this time, "dozens of saloons" in the city were attracting "hundreds of often rowdy drinkers, especially around the first of the month when pensioners at the nearby Soldiers Home [now the Veterans Administration complex on Wilshire] received their stipends."[59] Meanwhile watering holes in Santa Monica Canyon flouted what little regulation there was of saloons by serving alcohol at all hours and even on Sunday.

However, at the same time, residents who considered drinking immoral were rallying together and would soon take action to try to reclaim their city. A Santa Monica branch of the Woman's Christian Temperance Union was already at work in the 1880s. By 1895 the city had a "Prohibition Congregational Church" that presumably also denounced the evils of alcohol. Meanwhile Frederick H. Rindge, a transplanted New Englander and the wealthy owner of Malibu Ranch as well as a resident of the city, became the leader of the city's temperance forces. Their efforts turned temperance into a political issue that would not go away.

Santa Monica's 1900 election was the first time restricting alcohol was put to a vote in the city and it was a success for temperance advocates. At issue was whether Santa Monica would outlaw saloons within its limits. By a vote of 305 to 218, residents said "yes" though clearly the city was split on the issue. Passage of this measure was smoothed by the fact that Rindge, in his great dedication to the anti-saloon cause, pledged to give the city $2,500 of his own money to make up the $2,500 the city would lose in saloon licensing fees. The immediate result of the 1900 vote was that saloons, once so plentiful, were put out of business in Santa Monica. However, the anti-alcohol forces soon found that they had won the battle but not the war. To begin with, alcohol could still be sold because restaurants and hotels retained the right to serve drinks with meals costing over 25¢. In addition, restaurants and hotels sometimes violated this rule. Indeed, when some of Santa Monica's prominent citizens were convicted of purchasing alcohol without the requisite 25¢ meal, the rule was weakened to allow alcohol to be served as long as it came with some kind of food. As historians Wolf and Madar write,

"Soon 'restaurants' were dispensing soda crackers with every shot—and some got by with handing patrons an empty cracker box."[60]

Rindge and his forces were not about to give up however. Thanks to the Rindge-backed Good Government League, the 1902 election brought in an anti-saloon majority on the city's governing board of trustees and by 1903 voters were asked to decide on a total prohibition ordinance that would make Santa Monica an entirely "dry" city. The measure failed with 544 against and 287 in favor, proving that most residents were not ready for such a drastic step. The debate did not end there though. Prohibition was coming to a boil as a state and national issue and locally the *Outlook* lobbied for severe alcohol laws. In 1908 another prohibition measure made its way onto the ballot and was again voted down. Anti-alcohol forces did score a small victory when they succeeded in prohibiting alcohol on the new Santa Monica Pleasure Pier, but most everywhere else alcohol was flowing fairly freely. Only in 1917, after many tries, did the "bone-dry workers," as the *Outlook* called them, taste triumph when residents passed a law that prohibited the sale of intoxicating beverages in Santa Monica with 2,861 in favor and 1,407 opposed. In the very same year the city of Los Angeles passed a stringent anti-alcohol law of its own that allowed only beer and wine (not hard liquor) in restaurants, and only if served with meals. Southern Californians intent on getting drunk found their options drying up, though neighboring Venice was one holdout that remained "wet" until national prohibition began in 1919.

Just as before, however, the prohibitionists soon found that passing a law was one thing and living by it another. The truth was that even after 1917 in Los Angeles, and in Santa Monica as well, booze wasn't that hard to find. This fact was made obvious on the night before national prohibition was to begin on June 30, 1919. That night an estimated 100,000 revelers jammed into special three-car Pacific Electric trains or crowded into automobiles going to the amusement zones in Venice and Ocean Park to drink with abandon before the federal restrictions took effect. Clearly, though there were many in favor of restricting alcohol in Santa Monica, plenty of others were more than happy to sell or drink it.

Ironically, it seems that during Prohibition Santa Monica was more given over to vice than ever before. Private citizens made their own alcoholic concoctions at home and speakeasies abounded. In Santa Monica Canyon Doc Law's drugstore and soda fountain stocked prescription "elixirs" and sold illicit cocktails to those who knew the password. Sam's hamburger stand and the Golden Butterfly also sold alcohol in the canyon. In Santa Monica proper, hotels such as the Georgian on Ocean Avenue kept private rooms for their clients to enjoy drinks, and speakeasies could be found on the city's piers and elsewhere. More than one anecdote suggests that pliable officers of the law could be persuaded to wink at such operations. Meanwhile Santa Monica, as a beach community, served as a practical landing place for liquor destined for illegal sale throughout the Los Angeles area. Realistically, there was little chance of banishing alcohol in a place as dedicated to enjoyment as Santa Monica was in this era. By the 1920s, despite all laws to the contrary, Santa Monica's anti-alcohol forces had been vanquished and the city was open to plenty of illegal activity. For the moment at least many Santa Monicans were ready to tolerate law-breaking and corruption in their town. Indeed, in the 1930s this tolerance would extend to other vices such as gambling as well. It would take both government force and a renewed sense of public outrage to bring Santa Monica back to respectability.

As battles over the moral qualities of the city played out, Santa Monicans faced another extremely important question involving the city's identity: Would Santa Monica remain an independent city or would she be absorbed by her ever-expanding neighbor, Los Angeles? Los Angeles was, of course, growing much faster than Santa Monica. By 1920 Los Angeles boasted a population of 576,000 while Santa Monica had only 15,252 residents. Although Santa Monica derived benefits from having such a big city nearby—among them the fact that many Angelinos spent their money freely while in the city—such proximity posed risks to Santa Monica's independence as well, especially as Los Angeles increasingly spread westward from its original downtown core.

The issue of whether Santa Monica would remain independent came to a head over water. Water has always been a precious commodity in Southern California, and those who control it wield power. Los Angeles grasped this fact early on and by 1913 had completed an ambitious scheme to control water from the distant Owens River and have it delivered by aqueduct to Los Angeles. The city of Los Angeles, possessed by a powerful sense of territorial ambition, then used this water as a bargaining chip with neighboring towns and cities that did not have sufficient water resources to support their booming populations. Rather than sell surplus Owens Valley water to needy communities, Los Angeles decided that, as historian Kevin Starr has described:

> A community might have all the water it needed—provided that it became part of Los Angeles. Between 1913 and 1927 Los Angeles expanded itself through annexation into the largest metropolitan territory under a single government in the United States.[61]

This approach to city-building meant that as of 1930 Los Angeles was a monstrous 441.7 square miles in size. As one contemporary observer remarked, "The map of the city resembles nothing so much as an amoeba gone berserk."[62]

In these years, cities and unincorporated areas all around Santa Monica capitulated to Los Angeles, usually because they were unable to resist her offer of plentiful water. The "Westgate Tract," which adjoined Santa Monica Canyon on the west and north, was annexed in 1916 in return for a guaranteed water supply. Santa Monica Canyon itself decided to join with Los Angeles in 1924. (In a novel twist, Canyon annexation advocates argued that the Los Angeles school system would be preferable to what Santa Monica had provided.) Not long afterwards, in 1925, Venice voted away its municipality for the lack of an independent water supply. Other areas near Santa Monica, such as Sawtelle (once a distinct town) and Brentwood, were also absorbed into Los Angeles, with the result that Santa Monica, except for its Pacific side, grew to be entirely surrounded and effectively hemmed in by its behemoth neighbor.

The City Finds a Niche

Santa Monica made a different choice, in part because it had developed its own water sources early on. Before the town was founded in 1875 there were only two reliable sources of water in the area. One was the stream that ran through Santa Monica Canyon. The other, what came to be known as the San Vicente spring, was the same spring that the Portolá expedition found on its travels through the area in 1769 (located on the grounds of today's University High School in West Los Angeles). In the town's early years it was this spring that supplied settlers via a small reservoir and pipe system that brought water to Santa Monica. Once in the town, water was then distributed by tank wagons to individual homes and businesses. Later, iron water mains were installed throughout the city to distribute this water, but by the 1890s it was already clear that the San Vicente spring was inadequate for Santa Monica's growing population. In 1897 the Santa Monica Land and Water Company was formed to develop better sources of water. This company, owned largely by Senator Jones, then bought the water rights to thousands of acres of land in the Santa Monica Mountains, built reservoirs there, and delivered the water by pipes to the city. Other privately owned water companies, such as Frederick Rindge's Artesian Water Company, also served Santa Monica. However, water service was not optimal, especially in dry times when sometimes only a trickle of water would flow from faucets and supply was insufficient to sustain lawns and gardens.

Perhaps noting Los Angeles's great success in acquiring a reliable water supply, Santa Monicans decided by 1916 to create their own municipal water system. As such, they voted in favor of a bond issue that permitted the city to purchase several water companies and their facilities at a cost of $712,500. This was the first step towards water independence. In the same year city residents also considered annexation to Los Angeles and, after a heated debate in which the *Outlook* rallied readers to the cause of "home rule," decided against it. Despite efforts to take control of and improve the city's water supply, the explosive growth of Santa Monica's population, particularly in the 1920s, meant increasing pressure on available resources. The fact that the early 1920s were drought years intensified the crisis, causing residents to approve another bond measure, this time for $1 million to acquire water-bearing lands on Charnock Road in today's Mar Vista. The money also financed the construction of two new reservoirs, one at Bundy and Wilshire, and one on Franklin Hill near Santa Monica's northeastern boundary. The Charnock wells would become Santa Monica's main water source.

However, even as Santa Monica's independent water supply was being improved, a movement to surrender self-government and join Los Angeles gained steam. In August of 1924 more that 200 citizens, many in the real estate business, banded together to form an annexation association and began espousing the benefits of being part of Los Angeles. They complained that their homes received insufficient water, doubted that the Charnock wells could meet the city's needs, and looked forward to the day when, "We will boast that we live in the best end of the great city of Los Angeles." To those who feared the city might lose its distinctive identity, annexationists pointed to Hollywood, which they said had joined the great metropolis but had not lost its special flavor. With an election to decide the matter scheduled for December, feelings on both sides intensified and the debate reached a fevered pitch. A growing number of residents, led by Judge Fred E. Taft, began to resist the call to annexation, citing the virtues of independence. Eventually the *Outlook* joined the fray, with Editor Robert P. Holliday writing forcefully against annexation, which he equated with "strangulation" for the city. When one annexationist suggested that his side would continue putting annexation on the ballot until it passed, Holliday responded hotly, "We are in the fight to stay and . . . we shall never falter in our efforts to bring such idle threats to the surface and crush them back to earth again."[63] The outcome looked unsure up until election day and the campaigns held last-minute rallies and parades while the anti-consolidation forces even dropped pamphlets from airplanes.

In the end most Santa Monicans could not stomach becoming Angelinos and rejected annexation. But the vote, a record turnout with 4,555 against and 3,479 in favor, revealed just how divided the city had been on the subject. Soon the improved water service from the Charnock wells quelled discontent and the urge to join Los Angeles withered. Later in the 1920s Santa Monica insured its long-term water supply by joining with other cities, including Los Angeles, to form the Metropolitan Water District—a super-agency responsible for the financing and construction of the Colorado Aqueduct that would bring vast quantities of water to the Southland. Annexation was forgotten. The fact that Santa Monicans refused to pay for water with their independence has, of course, had a vast effect on life in the city ever since, allowing it to take a path quite different from that of Los Angeles on matters as diverse as schools, police, building regulations, and environmental policy.

By the 1920s Santa Monica had come into its own. In embracing leisure and tourism as its principle industries, the city found a more natural fit than the railroad and port ambitions of its founders. It also established itself in the national consciousness as a fascinating place where exciting things happened. In wrestling with moral questions like temperance, Santa Monicans attempted to reach a consensus on what type of city Santa Monica would be. The fact that no real agreement was reached hinted at the independent-mindedness of the city's inhabitants. This autonomous spirit was proven when the city rejected annexation to Los Angeles. In these years, many of the themes that would persist through the twentieth century and to the present—like dedication to sports, appreciation of the good life, and the tendency to take alternative political paths—were solidly established, giving the city a unique quality that made it both immensely appealing and different from other places. But there were troubles ahead, the Depression and World War II were not far off, and Santa Monicans would have to adapt themselves and their city to meet the changes.

Chapter Seven

THE DEPRESSION YEARS

The Great Depression threw a wet blanket on the high-flying prosperity of 1920s Santa Monica. The economy was bad and most everyone felt it. But the 1930s brought other hardships as well, including worsening vice problems in the city, a bad earthquake, and heightened racial tensions. In this difficult climate, the city worked hard to revive its struggling tourism industry, but ended up creating a white elephant instead—Santa Monica harbor. There were some bright spots though. Less contrived leisure attractions such as Muscle Beach offered thrills for participants and spectators alike that were easy on the pocket. And thanks to Douglas Aircraft Company, manufacturing gained a foothold in Santa Monica, helping to lift the city out of the Depression a few years before the rest of the country.

Hard times hit Santa Monica even before the great crash on Wall Street. Real estate prices ballooned unrealistically through the 1920s but faltered by 1927 and Santa Monica felt the brunt of it as people tightened their belts, cancelled beach club memberships, and spent less on frivolous diversions. Then in 1929, when the nation as a whole plunged deeply into financial crisis, Santa Monica followed helplessly. Almost immediately the city's banks were compromised as anxious citizens rushed to withdraw their cash. Unable to pay everyone, once solid institutions such as Bay Cities Guaranty Building and Loan Association and the Marine Bank in Ocean Park folded. Other banks survived, but business was bad and profits measly. Across the city quite a few businesses failed, their owners no longer able to make ends meet. Meanwhile building activity, always a mainstay of the economy in Southern California, plunged dramatically. Where the city had seen projects valued at $3 million begun in 1929, projects started in 1933 were valued at less that $500,000.

With stores closing and building down, Santa Monicans lost jobs. Indeed, by 1932 the city had 1,600 unemployed people, 800 of whom had families to support. In 1934 and 1935, 1,700 families were suffering enough to band together in an Unemployed Citizens League. A self-help organization, members worked to obtain surplus food and found odd jobs like woodcutting or clothes mending. They also fished to supplement their meals and even opened kitchens to serve those who were even worse off—the midwestern Dust Bowl migrants and poor from the South who came to California to escape the agricultural crises devastating their regions. Santa Monica's unemployed received help from their more fortunate neighbors as well. In 1932, for example, city employees decided to donate part of their pay to unemployment relief. Organizations such as the Community Chest also raised funds to help those hardest hit by the Depression.

It did not help that in one of the worst years of the Depression in Southern California a major earthquake hit. Southern California's boosters had long denied that earthquakes were a real threat to the region, but the March 10, 1933 earthquake, centered at Long Beach, made a mockery of such claims. Measuring 6.3 on the Richter scale, the quake struck at 5:54 p.m. and lasted ten seconds—long enough to kill fifty-two people and do an estimated $40 million in damage in the Los Angeles area. In Santa Monica the worst casualties were the city's schools, many of which were too damaged to use and remained so for several years. As a result, in the depths of the Depression, many Santa Monica school children attended classes in tents set up on school grounds until money from federal New Deal programs helped rebuild structures later in the decade.

For Santa Monica's racial minorities, intolerance added another layer of misery to these lean years. Black Santa Monicans continued to be treated as second-class citizens. As Lloyd Allen, a newcomer in 1939 from Shreveport, Louisiana, later recalled, there were no signs segregating whites and blacks but "it was understood . . . you just didn't do certain things." Those things included eating at most restaurants, sitting among whites at movie theatres, or working alongside whites as equals in many stores and businesses. Conditions were perhaps better than in the South but, as Lloyd Allen remembered, there was certainly "more hypocrisy here."[64]

Competition for jobs made some white Santa Monicans less hospitable than ever to their African-American, Hispanic, or Asian neighbors. Joaquin de la Peña, a native-born Santa Monican and descendant of an early ranching family, saw prejudice increase as whites told him, "Why don't you go back where you came from?"[65] Indeed, the Hispanic population, swelled by Mexicans who had migrated starting around 1910, faced increasing hostility during the Depression for "taking jobs from Americans," with the result that over 13,000 Mexicans were forcibly repatriated from Los Angeles County in the 1930s. Meanwhile, though Santa Monicans generally treated Asians amicably, Asians sometimes encountered prejudice. In one case, the white owner of a gas station on Pico Boulevard tried to increase his business, and cut into that of a gas station owned by a Japanese-American nearby, by erecting a large sign urging motorists to "Buy from a White Man."

As individual Santa Monicans were struggling through these various hardships, the city as a whole faced its own challenges as it slid down the slippery slope of vice and corruption in the 1930s. Prohibition had already done much to erode lawful respectability in 1920s Santa Monica, but even after Prohibition was repealed in 1933 a climate of tolerance for illicit activity endured. In Raymond Chandler's hardboiled detective novels of the era, which accurately detailed so much of the Southland's seamy side, "Bay City" (Santa Monica) was "probably no crookeder than Los Angeles." Unfortunately, that wasn't saying much because vice and corruption reached epidemic proportions in 1930s Los Angeles.[66]

Santa Monica certainly had a prostitution problem. A high-class brothel run by well-known madam Lee Frances (who also had houses in San Francisco and Los

Angeles) was operating on the 2300 block of La Mesa Drive in the late 1930s, apparently with little interference from the police and was probably just the tip of the iceberg. But gambling was a much more visible problem and stories abound of its prevalence in Depression-era Santa Monica. A few examples suggest the ubiquity of gambling in the city. The Casa del Mar beach club, known for its respectable business and professional members, had illegal slot machines in the 1930s. Posing as fundraisers for charity, racketeers ran illegal card games in Santa Monica restaurants while police turned a blind eye. Meanwhile, bookmakers set up shop in hotel rooms and bingo parlors flourished in Ocean Park where occasional police raids were apparently intended more to keep up the flow of payments to authorities than to stop the gambling. Although seemingly innocuous, these activities were subject to control by gangsters and syndicates who were anything but. And when these nefarious elements used their money to influence politicians and police, ordinary citizens were the losers.

By far the most flagrant gambling operation was not actually in the city but just over three miles off Santa Monica pier in international waters. This was the infamous *Rex* gambling ship run by Tony Cornero, one of four such ships he anchored off the Southern California coast in the 1930s. Cornero was an accomplished bootlegger in Los Angeles during Prohibition, dominating the trade there with the help of his brother Frank. A trip to prison and the repeal of Prohibition sidelined Cornero's liquor operations, so he created a new and lucrative niche fixing up ships as luxurious floating casinos and welcoming patrons who arrived by water taxi. The *Rex* was in service in Santa Monica Bay by May of 1938 and Cornero advertised the fact on the radio and in newspapers. Open twenty-four hours a day, this paradise for gamblers offered roulette, blackjack, craps, keno, poker, faro, and other games along with first-class food and liquor served by white-jacketed waiters. It easily accommodated thousands of patrons who arrived via a fleet of small boats from the pier.

But not everyone enjoyed the *Rex* or the climate of a city wide open to crime in the 1930s and Santa Monicans fought back in various ways. An initiative was passed in 1933 banning games of chance on Ocean Park's piers. Charles Warren, an editor of the *Outlook* for many years, reported that around this time there was "strong popular feeling" against gambling. As a result, voters elected Mayor Claude C. Crawford, based on "a reform platform with a pledge to enforce the law against gambling."[67] Meanwhile, citizens' groups such as the PTA expressed outrage and helped pressure the city to do something about the *Rex*. Attempts were also made to shut down the water taxi business so essential to the *Rex*'s success. Meanwhile, the *Outlook* ran stories emphasizing the human tragedy associated with gambling. One story told of Emilio Gutierrez, a World War I veteran and cook who had lost his wife and daughter. Gutierrez, the *Outlook* reported, was lured to the *Rex* by its ads promising "thrills and gaiety," but instead of fun Gutierrez lost his life savings. Unwisely he resorted to forging a check to try to win back his money. In the end, Gutierrez said, "Tony got my money" while Gutierrez himself got a trip to San Quentin on forgery charges.[68] For a time public pressure caused Cornero to move the *Rex* south of Santa Monica, but he later returned. Around this same time, Santa Monicans collected 250 signatures on a petition against gambling. However, gambling interests demonstrated their influence by collecting 4,900 signatures (each at a cost of 10¢) on a pro-gambling petition presented to the city at the same time.

Indeed, it took a lot more than local will to close the *Rex*. It was not until the State of California, under the orders of Attorney General Earl Warren, sent over 300 men to raid Cornero's ships on August 2, 1939, that the *Rex* closed down. Cornero defended the *Rex* with fire hoses and armed guards declaring, "We are on the high seas and it's our own business whether we stay here one day—or ten years." But he eventually surrendered and the so-called "Battle of Santa Monica Bay" came to an end.[69] Warren announced triumphantly, "The banner of decency has been unfurled over these ships of chance" and, indeed, the closing of this blatant emporium of vice did restore some respectability to Santa Monica.[70] By the late 1940s the city had been cleaned up even more. Even so, other forms of gambling persisted in diverse forms. As late as 1964 the *Outlook* was still lamenting that "Gambling in every imaginable form has plagued the city in the last half-century."[71]

As Santa Monica grappled with vice, it was also struggling to maintain its place as a leisure destination, with mixed results. Movie stars continued to lend glamour to the city through the 1930s, and the long list of resident celebrities included Greta Garbo, Claudette Colbert, Shirley Temple, Joan Crawford, Clark Gable, Carole Lombard, Mickey Rooney, Barbara Stanwyck, Bette Davis, Gary Cooper, Cary Grant, Betty Grable, Fred MacMurray, and many, many more. Their world of fancy parties and sumptuous homes was largely insulated from the ravages of the Depression.

But most ordinary people had a lot less money to spend and Santa Monica's leisure industry suffered for it. Many of the lavish beach clubs that had been a mainstay of beach culture in the 1920s closed their doors as their members now balked at high fees. The Casa del Mar was one of the few that stayed open. When the 1932 Olympic Games were held in Los Angeles, Santa Monica hoped to attract visitors with a promotional brochure touting the city as "the recognized leader in beauty, culture, refinement and high class recreation." The same brochure directed visitors to the Crystal Pier solarium at the foot of Hollister Street, endorsed by "famous war correspondent" Floyd Gibbons. Gibbons enthused, "I'm a son of a gun for the sun . . . I've taken nude sun baths all over the globe from Timbuctoo to Moscow, but I've never found the sun better than right here in Santa Monica."

Despite such ringing endorsements, business remained mostly slow in the early 1930s. Amusement pier operators were short on cash to make improvements or install new attractions, and some older features closed down. Santa Monica Pier was in especially dire straits and its operator, the Santa Monica Amusement Company, was forced to declare bankruptcy in 1935. The once vibrant pier then entered a lengthy period of limbo under bank ownership. As the Depression dragged on, the grand La Monica Ballroom was downgraded into a convention center and offices, and then later into a roller-skating rink. Hopeful entrepreneurs attempted to bring some life to the pier by starting regular boat service to Catalina Island, but lack of interest ended that enterprise only months after it began. More successful was the sport fishing business. Locals and visitors fished off the pier, made use of several offshore barges anchored in the bay, or purchased excursions in small fishing boats leaving from the pier. Meanwhile, in Ocean Park the amusement trade was also falling off, its glory days as a seaside resort slipping away.

In this difficult economic climate the city took a gamble of its own—pursuing a plan to attract wealthy pleasure-seekers back to Santa Monica by building an expensive breakwater and yacht harbor. The idea of building a breakwater and harbor had been floated by various business and civic groups in the 1920s but had always floundered. In the 1930s the city, clinging to Santa Monica's reputation as the aristocrat of beach towns, took up the cause and began rallying citizen support through a publicity campaign of pamphlets, posters, billboards, and stickers. The plan was to build a 2,000-foot "crib-type" concrete wall 2,200 feet from shore that would create a calm anchorage for hundreds of pleasure boats. Agreeing with the plan and voting 5,429 to 1,925 in favor of a bond issue to fund construction, Santa Monicans were convinced that:

> Its nearness to Los Angeles, Hollywood and Beverly Hills, districts in which live a large number of wealthy residents who are interested in boats; its accessibility by way of beautiful Wilshire Boulevard . . . and the ease with which boat owners will be able to launch their craft from the new harbor are factors expected to dot beautiful Santa Monica Bay with sailing craft of every description from catboats built and owned by college students to majestic yachts which will sail the seven seas.[72]

Unfortunately, from the planning stages to completion the breakwater was plagued by problems. First, the city had difficulty getting bids for the construction. Then, once construction began, the original design had to be abandoned when it became clear that powerful ocean currents made crib-type construction impossible. The mistake was only realized after the first 2,000-ton concrete crib was put in place, only to crack into two useless pieces days later. After this costly mistake the city elected to spend the funds that remained on a simple rock mound seawall. By July 1934, the modified breakwater was completed. In all, some 200,000 tons of rocks from Catalina Island had been dumped into the bay and $690,000 from the bond issue was spent.

Although the breakwater did not turn out as initially planned, officials were nonetheless optimistic it would be a popular magnet for well-to-do visitors. A festive Regatta Week, held in August of 1934 and featuring congratulatory speeches by Mayor William Carter and other officials as well as yacht races, dances, and fireworks, seemed to bode well for the harbor's future. This confidence was misplaced. Over the years that followed it became clear the harbor was inconvenient to yachtsmen and women because there were no boat-side docks. (Instead people had to take small boats from the pier to reach their vessels). Worse, the breakwater disrupted the natural currents of the bay with two bad results. On the beach inside the harbor (to the north), sand was piling up at a significant rate, interfering with leisure activities there. Meanwhile, on the beaches south of the breakwater sand was disappearing, robbing establishments like the Casa del Mar, as well as ordinary beachgoers, of valued territory. By the late 1930s the city was embroiled in lengthy lawsuits with those who claimed losses due to either beach erosion or accretion. And even though the city never made money on the harbor, maintenance costs mounted. As early as 1939 the breakwater was already deteriorating and the city had spent and would continue to spend thousands upon thousands of dollars in a futile attempt to dredge the sand that was constantly invading the harbor. Then with the outbreak of World War II, pleasure craft were prohibited from leaving the harbor for security reasons. For all intents and purposes the harbor was a failure.

Ironically, while the city spent large sums in an effort to attract elite visitors, it was a spontaneous and free attraction—an area just south of the pier that was later dubbed "Muscle Beach"—that really generated enthusiasm and brought fun-seekers to Santa Monica during the Depression. It all started in the early 1930s when a few young gymnasts as well as circus and vaudeville performers started coming down to the Santa Monica Beach Playground looking for "a soft place to land" while practicing routines. The popularity of this spot increased when the city, in conjunction with the federal Works Progress Administration (WPA), added a small tumbling platform. Before long regulars were congregating daily for "some relief" from bleak times as they honed their athletic skills to the delight of increasingly large crowds of spectators.[73] In 1936 a large wooden platform was built and high rings and parallel bars were added. Soon crowds swelled into the thousands on weekends, creating traffic jams nearby and overflow on the boardwalk. Onlookers were thrilled by gymnastic feats and tumbling as performers flew on the rings, constructed human pyramids, and devised ever more complex and difficult stunts—and it was all free. By the late 1930s the beautifully honed bodies on display there, both male and female, inspired the name "Muscle Beach," and millions of people were coming to see what the excitement was all about, helping to transform the area just south of the pier into one of the most famous strips of beach in the world.

Southern California had long been devoted to sports, but Muscle Beach took fitness to another level. From the 1930s until its demise in 1958, Muscle Beach set trends that later spread across the nation. To begin with, it helped launch fitness innovators such as Vic Tanny, "considered by many to be the father of the modern gym chain," according to Muscle Beach expert Marla Rose, and Joe Gold, a bodybuilder from east Los Angeles who would later open the world-renowned Gold's Gyms.[74] Jack LaLanne, who amazed spectators by doing 1,000 push-ups in a row at Muscle Beach, as well as lifting weights and performing stunts no one else could top, later became famous as a fitness guru who would popularize exercise on television. Harold Zinkin, called "the Henry Ford of fitness" for his later invention of the Universal Gym Machine, was another pioneer who got his start at Muscle Beach.

The fact that women participated at Muscle Beach, performing feats of strength and agility surpassing what many men were capable of, was nothing short of revolutionary. Although amazing female athletes like Abbye "Pudgy" Stockton, a native Santa Monican, and Relna Brewer were sometimes heckled and jeered by male spectators, one female participant noted that, "I think Muscle Beach changed a lot of people's ideas of what women could do given the opportunity."[75] Certainly the women attracted a lot of publicity. Appearing in hundreds of magazine and newspaper articles published around the world, as well as in newsreels shown in theatres nationwide, they showed not only what women could achieve athletically but also, and not incidentally of course, demonstrated how attractive fit women could be.

The cult of the body developed at Muscle Beach, aided by weightlifting, would also spawn another innovation—the entirely new sport of bodybuilding. Gymnastics and tumbling were the main activities at Muscle Beach in the 1930s, but it wasn't long before "physical culturists," who aimed to sculpt their bodies to aesthetic perfection, became an important element there too. As such, Muscle Beach became a center for the emerging sport of bodybuilding and was a training ground for men like Armand Tanny, a Mr. America winner, and George Eiferman, a Mr. America and Mr. Universe winner. Their exploits would help popularize bodybuilding in mainstream America.

Thanks to Muscle Beach, Santa Monica, less through planning than serendipity, remained on the cutting edge of leisure during the Depression and continued its tradition of excellence in sports. But places like Muscle Beach were not money makers. Fortunately for Santa Monica, industry—notably aviation—finally took an important place beside leisure and tourism as a mainstay of the local economy in the 1930s. While Santa Monica had been a distinctly non-industrial place up until the 1930s—a map of the Los Angeles area in 1924 showed no industries in the city with more than twenty-five employees—the growth of Douglas Aircraft Company changed that even as the Depression stymied most other industries.

Donald Douglas made a name for himself in the 1920s as a brilliant aviation pioneer headquartered at what is now Douglas Park. His early successes led to expansion and a move to facilities adjacent to the already existing runways at Clover Field (today's Santa Monica Airport). Business was rather slow in the early 1930s, but an order from TWA for commercial passenger planes had the Douglas plant humming by 1933. Indeed, the advanced all-metal, twin-engine plane designed for TWA, the DC-1 (or Douglas Commercial-1) was an instant success. Its speed and quality helped TWA capture the lead in air travel from its rival United Airlines. TWA also purchased about 200 DC-2s, a refined version of the DC-1, keeping the Douglas plant busy through the mid-1930s. Continually making improvements, Douglas rolled out what many aviation experts consider to be the prototype of modern passenger aircraft—the immortal DC-3. The DC-3 was the plane that introduced many Americans to flying, carrying 95 percent of civilian travelers in the United States by 1937. Such was the dominance of Douglas and its DC-3 that in 1939 almost 90 percent of world air traffic was on DC-3s. With this phenomenal success employment in the Douglas plant grew dramatically from 965 workers in 1933 to 4,300 in 1936.

Despite additional hiring, in the summer of 1940 Douglas Aircraft had so many backlogged orders—$140 million worth—it began to operate around the clock. By this time Douglas was supplying not only civilian aircraft, but also military planes for France and England, who were already facing the threat of Hitler's Germany. Indeed, though the United States would not enter World War II until after Pearl Harbor on December 7, 1941, Douglas Aircraft was already shifting to war production mode in response to a request from President Roosevelt that American aviation firms step up production dramatically to 50,000 planes a year. On the eve of war Los Angeles County, home to six major aviation firms, had 113,000 men and women building planes, up from 13,000 in January of 1939. Thus while the Depression dragged on through the late 1930s in many parts of the United States, the fortunes of both Los Angeles and Santa Monica brightened several years earlier, thanks in large part to the vibrancy of Douglas Aircraft Company. As home to such a vital industry, Santa Monica was poised to play a crucial role in war production once the United States joined the fighting.

Douglas was a great asset to the city's economy in the 1930s but other smaller businesses contributed to economic recovery as well. Merle Norman founded a cosmetics firm in the city in 1931, with headquarters in a stylish Streamline Moderne building at 2525 Main Street. Thanks to innovative marketing techniques, her company prospered despite hard times. Other new businesses such as the W.I. Simonson Packard dealership on Seventeenth and Wilshire (now Simonson Mercedes-Benz) opened during the Depression as well. Meanwhile some older businesses transformed themselves to meet changing times. Santa Monica Brick Company, with a factory at Twenty-third Street (now Cloverfield) and Michigan Avenue, produced thousands of bricks a day in the late 1920s. In the 1930s the company turned to making decorative tile to adorn furniture under the name Taylor Tilery. Their striking Depression-era designs are now prized by collectors.

The local economy also got a boost from federal New Deal programs that funneled money into the city for numerous public works projects. After the 1933 Long Beach earthquake damaged many city schools, the WPA employed 1,400 men and spent almost $3 million of both federal money and local bond funds fixing and expanding Franklin and John Muir schools. Adams, Roosevelt, Washington, and Grant schools were so badly damaged that they were demolished and rebuilt from scratch. Santa Monica Pier was redecked as a WPA project around 1940. Several of the city's architectural gems were also made possible by New Deal programs. The central Post Office on Fifth Street, a monument to Art Deco Moderne style architecture, was a Public Works Administration project completed in 1937. The Santa Monica Civic Auditorium (Barnum Hall Theatre), on the grounds of Santa Monica High School, was built in 1938 as a WPA Project. Stanton Macdonald-Wright, a well-known Santa Monica artist, directed a team of WPA artisans to produce the striking curtain mural and mosaic there. The city also took advantage of federal funds to build a new city hall, which opened in 1939 on land considered blighted due to its run-down residences and businesses. These and other smaller projects helped keep Santa Monicans employed and the city afloat when most private building was curtailed due to the Depression.

Santa Monicans fought the Depression in many ways: by attempting to revive the leisure industry, by expanding older businesses such as Douglas Aircraft or founding new ones, and by accepting federal funds. There was one thing, however, that Santa Monicans refused to do for money even when times were tough—allow oil exploration and drilling within the city. Los Angeles had seen a massive oil boom in the 1920s as new wells at Huntington Beach, Long Beach, and elsewhere began pumping out thousands of barrels a day. Around this time oil speculators also worked to develop wells in Santa Monica and a few rigs were built, including one on Franklin Hill near Wilshire Boulevard and Stanford Street. However, these early projects fizzled. Then oil was discovered in neighboring Venice in 1929 and, by the early 1930s, that once picturesque town had become an unsightly oil field. Where lawns and gardens had once flourished, derricks, storage tanks, and drilling equipment marred the land. Though some property owners made a tidy profit on oil, quite a few residents lost money on unprofitable investments. Worse, they found their beachside town decline into an ugly and undesirable place to live. Perhaps because of this example, Santa Monicans voted in 1939 to prohibit all oil drilling within the city limits and the waters of Santa Monica Bay immediately offshore. The desire to preserve the city's scenic beauty played an important role in this vote. Having rejected annexation to Los Angeles in the 1920s, Santa Monicans were already proving in the 1930s that they would make different choices than their larger neighbor—in this case placing preservation of beauty over profits from oil.

The 1930s in Santa Monica were a trying time. With unemployment, vice, racial intolerance, natural disaster, and a stalled leisure industry all eroding the quality of life in the city, it looked for a while like the good times would never return. In a sense it was true. By the time the Depression started to loosen its grip on the city it was already clear that the breezy party atmosphere of the 1920s was gone for good. Indeed, as the 1940s began, war loomed on the horizon and the humming Douglas Aircraft plant was a harbinger of what was to come. Once World War II broke out there would be more jobs than people to fill them, more growth than the city could handle, and more excitement than anyone wanted. The city that changed during the Depression to meet the challenges of a bad economy would change a great deal more before peace was restored in 1945.

Chapter Eight

LIFE DURING WARTIME

Santa Monica in the 1930s was still a city on the periphery. Though beloved by its inhabitants, it was but a small city next to the larger and more important Los Angeles metropolis. And Los Angeles was itself provincial and peripheral to the more established industrial cities of the East. The Southland had certainly shown phenomenal growth but it was not yet taken seriously as an important region making a vital contribution to the nation's economy or well-being. All that changed with World War II. Suddenly Santa Monica and the Los Angeles area generally were in the thick of the action, not only as a nexus of war production but as a potential target for enemy assailants, and what happened here mattered a great deal to the rest of the nation. Under pressure as a strategically important area, Santa Monica experienced air raids, feverish industrial activity, a massive influx of newcomers, changed race and gender relations, and yet more adaptation of its leisure industry. Through this crisis Santa Monica and her residents were changed indelibly—quaint Santa Monica was gone, at least for a time, and an industrial powerhouse teeming with newcomers had taken her place.

Many of the war's changes would unfold over time, but others came with remarkable swiftness as people responded to the shocking Japanese attack on Pearl Harbor of December 7, 1941. Indeed, a sense of safety and complacency was the first casualty of the war as fear gripped the city. Residents of Santa Monica had particular reason to worry. Santa Monica's position on the Pacific coast put it within striking range of the Japanese. As home to Douglas Aircraft, which was already supplying vital aircraft to the U.S. military, it seemed to be an especially likely target for attack. Santa Monica resident Charles Warren recalled:

> The first few days—and especially nights—after the daring sky invasion of American domain were nightmares. There were constant reports of approaching enemy warships and warplanes and cities along the Pacific Coast were on a constant alert.[76]

Although in retrospect we know that the West Coast was relatively safe from attack, this was far from obvious at the time. As state librarian Kevin Starr has written, "the attack on Pearl Harbor, so swift, so lethally effective . . . sustained fears, which soon became convictions, that the Japanese, having launched such a bold attack, were quite logically en route to the Coast."[77]

Given the apparent vulnerability of Santa Monica and other nearby cities, officials and residents lost no time in organizing defenses to ward off attacks. The Army swung into action almost immediately. Due to heightened tensions before Pearl Harbor, a Coast Artillery regiment had already been conducting maneuvers in Santa Monica, and they were quickly enlisted to guard and defend the Douglas plant at Clover Field. Extra private security guards hired by Douglas later joined them. After the United States officially declared war on both Japan and Germany, the Army sent additional troops to protect the city from attack or invasion. Navy and Coast Guard vessels patrolled Santa Monica Bay on the lookout for suspicious activity on the water. In addition, barrage balloons were launched to hinder air attacks, and anti-aircraft guns and artillery were deployed along the coast to shoot down enemy planes.

Meanwhile, the city quickly took steps to ensure Santa Monicans' safety. Firefighters and police were put on longer shifts and all leave was cancelled for these essential personnel. Roadblocks were set up around the Douglas factory to enhance security there. The harbor foghorn was pressed into use as an air-raid siren and mounted atop city hall. And residents were told to prepare for the worst in an air assault by filling bathtubs with water, shutting off gas appliances, and keeping buckets of sand outside their homes to fight incendiary attacks. The Red Cross pitched in by setting up a first-aid station in Santa Monica to handle any who might be injured in a Japanese attack. And Santa Monicans, appalled by the carnage in Hawaii, began to rally to the nation's defense by enlisting in the armed services. On December 8 the local Navy recruiting station reported a "flood" of prospective recruits when eighteen men flocked there before 11:00 a.m. For those who did not enlist there were opportunities to serve at home. Civil defense groups, which included women as well as men, were organized soon after the war began and were charged with tasks such as manning stations to monitor the coast and enforcing wartime regulations.

Blackouts, which began almost immediately after Pearl Harbor, added to the feeling that war had truly come to Santa Monica. The first blackout was ordered on December 8 in response to a warning that sixty enemy planes were menacing the West Coast. Luckily it was a false alarm because, unaccustomed to the blackout routine, Santa Monicans left quite a few lights on. Spurred by panic and anger, some residents did try to increase compliance by smashing the lights of downtown businesses left on at the close of the day. Nightly blackouts were instituted starting on December 10, and with that Santa Monicans had more chance to practice, as well as install dark coverings over windows and cover their car headlights with cellophane, tape, or paint to minimize their glow. To increase compliance, civil defense wardens patrolled neighborhoods enforcing blackout rules and the city instituted a penalty of $500 and six months in jail for anyone failing to extinguish lights.

Even though Santa Monicans prepared, the first several months of the war did little to reduce the fear that a Japanese attack was imminent. On Christmas Eve of 1941, for example, the American lumber ship *Absaroka* was torpedoed by a Japanese submarine not far from Catalina Island. The ship did not sink but the message was clear—Japanese submarines were a silent but lurking menace in the waters off Southern California. Another disquieting incident occurred on February 23, 1942, when a Japanese vessel shelled the oil storage area at Ellwood, twelve miles north of Santa Barbara. Then, on the night of February 24, 1942, the whole Los Angeles area was thrown into a panic by a warning from Army officials that an unidentified aircraft had been sighted over Los Angeles. By the wee hours of February 25 a blackout had been ordered, and at 3:12 a.m. anti-aircraft units of Los Angeles's Coast Artillery began firing their weapons into the pitch-black sky, struggling to beat back what they thought was an invasion of hostile aircraft. In the hour that followed, 1,430 shells were fired by the U.S. military, air-raid sirens wailed, searchlights raked the sky scanning the blackness for the attackers, and anti-aircraft barrages exploded in the air along the coast. In the end, there were no attackers and an errant weather balloon was probably the "unidentified aircraft" that had touched off the whole affair. The only things that hit the ground in Santa Monica and other coastal communities were duds and shrapnel from American guns, and the only deaths that occurred were due to heart attacks and car accidents. Nevertheless, the "Battle of Los Angeles," as it came to be known, increased apprehension and brought a real sense of war home for Southern Californians.

In the atmosphere of panic that marked the early months of the war, edgy Southern Californians saw danger everywhere and increasingly suspected their Japanese-American neighbors of spying and collaborating with the enemy. Indeed, immediately after Pearl Harbor Japanese Americans in Santa Monica faced hostility. On December 8, for example, before other civilian boat traffic was curtailed, Santa Monica's harbormaster, Sam Reed, refused to allow a group of Japanese-American fishermen to leave the harbor, suspicious of their motives. This rising hostility caught Santa Monica's Japanese-American community by surprise, especially because they had been well accepted in Santa Monica for decades.

The Japanese had long been a fixture in Santa Monica, their presence dating back to the late nineteenth century when a Japanese fishing village had been established near the Long Wharf. The village was dismantled by 1920, but some Japanese stayed in Santa Monica, newcomers arrived, and over time a community grew. Around 1940 the Japanese-American community was well-integrated into the life of Santa Monica with families dispersed around the city, mixing with whites as equals, rather than concentrated in an ethnic enclave. Many Japanese-American men worked as contract gardeners, landscape contractors, or nursery owners. Others owned small produce businesses, such as the Tanaka fruit and vegetable stand on Montana Avenue, or laundromats. Numbering about 400 in 1940, the Japanese-American population was cohesive enough to support a school where their children went after school for instruction in Japanese language and culture. The school, located at 1824 Sixteenth Street, also served as the center of social life for Japanese-American Santa Monicans, as well as a place for organizing picnics, Christmas parties, plays, and other events. An all-Japanese church, the Free Methodist Church on Twelfth Street (Interstate

10 now runs over the site), founded in 1925, ministered to the spiritual needs of Christians in the community, while Buddhists went to neighboring Los Angeles for worship. Although Santa Monica's Japanese Americans continued to maintain some of the traditions of their ancestral land, they only rarely experienced racial intolerance before the war. As Kaz Yamamoto, a pre-war resident of Santa Monica put it, "the whole community of Santa Monica were nice to Japanese."[78]

Despite this amicable pre-war situation, the public mood shifted quickly after Pearl Harbor as panic replaced rational thinking. As historian Dana Blakemore put it, Santa Monica's Japanese Americans became "enemies overnight." Immediately after Pearl Harbor the FBI began arresting Japanese Americans in West Los Angeles and Venice on suspicion of sabotage, and Japanese Americans in Santa Monica and elsewhere had weapons, cameras, and radios confiscated. Politicians and newspapers, including the *Los Angeles Times* and Santa Monica's own *Outlook*, helped fan the flames of anti-Japanese sentiment. Citing the impossibility of distinguishing between loyal Japanese Americans and subversives, an early 1942 editorial in the *Outlook* called for the evacuation of all citizens of Japanese ancestry from the area. One white Santa Monican, Victoria Lang, described the ominous mood of the time:

> It was a really blurred period, between all the drama of all the blackouts and the darkness . . . It was that kind of—both a sense of patriotism and a sense of fear—terror of what was going to happen next . . . My husband was employed by Douglas Aircraft that was right up the street and he just absorbed the general attitude which was hotly anti-Japanese. He was not that angry a man . . . but would quote others as very, very vengeful, and that they [the Japanese] should not have been allowed to come into America and therefore threaten us, and all the kind of bigotry that comes out of general ignorance.[79]

Amidst this growing hysteria, Santa Monica's Japanese Americans tried to defend their loyalty. Very soon after Pearl Harbor, a large rally for all Santa Monicans was held at the Municipal Auditorium. On a program including patriotic readings of the Bill of Rights and the Gettysburg Address by white participants, fourteen Japanese Americans from the local community added their own patriotic message, declaring "We are American citizens. We declare our absolute loyalty to our country. We declare our purpose to faithfully fulfill all our obligations and to defend the United States against all aggressors."[80] Putting these words into action, Japanese-American community leaders soon actively organized the community in loyal activities. In early 1942, for example, 107 Japanese Americans in Santa Monica enrolled in Red Cross training classes to help defend their American homeland, while others contributed money to the Red Cross or pledged to buy defense bonds.

Tragically, it was not enough to stem the rising tide of intolerance. Thanks in part to public pressure from Californians, President Franklin Roosevelt issued Executive

Order 9066 on February 19, 1942, ordering the evacuation of all Japanese, whether American citizens or not, from the West Coast. By March of 1942 some 2,000 Japanese in California, many of them community leaders, had been arrested and detained by the U.S. Justice Department. Those who were not arrested—including all women and children—were forced to quickly settle their affairs before being incarcerated in one of several hastily prepared internment camps. Santa Monica's Japanese Americans went to Manzanar—a desolate spot in the Owens Valley.

With such short notice it was difficult to sell businesses or belongings, or find someone to look after homes. Some Japanese Americans in Santa Monica had to abandon their property. Yosh Ando, the owner of a produce market at Fourth and Pico was one who, unable to find a buyer for his enterprise, lost everything. Others were forced to sell at low prices. A few fared better and managed to hang on to property through the war, aided by sympathetic whites. One family, the Tsutsumiuchis, decided to voluntarily relocate to Colorado to avoid being sent to Manzanar. On very short notice they packed only clothes while a Jewish neighbor, Mrs. Ray Lane, purchased their train tickets and got them safely to Union Station. Afterwards, Mrs. Lane helped put their home in order, settled accounts, and sold excess belongings, sending the money to the family in Colorado. Another man, Henry Tsurutani, was able to rent his home to a family that conscientiously paid him $30 in rent every month, sending it to Manzanar.

Overall, however, removal and internment during World War II was a disaster for Santa Monica's Japanese-American community. No cases of anti-American, subversive activity were ever documented among the Japanese-American residents of the West Coast, yet they were deprived of their rights as citizens, suffered huge economic damage, were cut off from ordinary jobs and social life, and were effectively imprisoned for the duration of the war. Although after the war some would return to try to reconstruct their old lives in Santa Monica, many Japanese-Americans would never recoup the losses, whether emotional or economic, sustained during this devastating time.

For the rest of Santa Monica, of course, Japanese evacuation eased fears and allowed people to go on with the business of working and living in wartime. Increasingly this meant working at the Douglas Aircraft plant, which quickly became the focal point of life in wartime Santa Monica. As one wartime resident remembered, "It consumed the community—everybody was somehow connected to Douglas Aircraft."[81] Douglas had already begun operating around the clock and expanding capacity even before the war began. Now, with the United States engaged in a conflict of epic proportions, turning out large numbers of military planes became a matter of the utmost urgency and Douglas responded by vastly increasing hiring, expanding the original Santa Monica plant (as well as adding operations at several other Douglas facilities in Los Angeles), and exceeding all pre-war production records. In this effort Douglas was supported by the federal government, which not only dispensed huge contracts (the United States ordered more than $7 billion in aircraft during the war), but also worked to smooth over labor problems, helped coordinate delivery of vital materials, and instituted programs to increase worker productivity.

Santa Monica was not alone in its focus on aircraft production during the war. In fact, what happened in the city was a microcosm of what was happening in the entire Los Angeles area. During the war the aircraft industry was the dominant industry in the Southland, not only because of Douglas, but because many important firms including Lockheed, Northrop, Vega, Convair, and North American were also located here. In addition to these giants there were, by 1944, an estimated 4,000 companies of all sizes, including a number in Santa Monica, involved in war production with the vast majority related to aviation. Thus, as Santa Monica was transformed into an industrial city driven by aviation, Los Angeles made a similar transition from industrial backwater to crucial hub of the defense industry, a role that it would keep after the war ended.

The transformation at Douglas Aircraft in Santa Monica was dramatic indeed. From 7,589 workers in 1939, Douglas grew to employ an astonishing 33,000 men and women by 1944. (More than 160,000 were employed by Douglas in all six of the company's Los Angeles area plants). And to accommodate all these workers the plant had to expand. In 1941 the municipal golf course next to Clover Field was taken over by Douglas operations. In addition, the airport was extended over an adjacent residential area that had been cleared by picking up and moving houses to other locations in the city. Aware that such a behemoth factory would present an easy target for enemy bombers, windows were painted over to reduce the visibility of the powerful floodlights that illuminated the factory at night. Authorities then enlisted landscape architect Edward Huntsman-Trout to devise an ingenious camouflage for the exterior. His design turned the area over the massive Douglas plant into a realistic replica of a typical Santa Monica residential neighborhood, made more authentic looking by mock houses, trees, and cars. A decoy plant was even built nearby to further mislead potential bombers.

Of course, the peaceful-looking camouflage job contrasted greatly with what actually went on inside Douglas. The plant never stopped humming, operating three shifts a day, seven days a week, packed with workers whose productivity soared during the war because everything was organized, both time and materials, to reduce waste. The work itself was, of course, streamlined, but Douglas also took care to provide a huge cafeteria where hearty subsidized meals ensured workers were well nourished in a time of food rationing. At breaks Douglas offered morale-boosting treats such as free Eskimo Pie ice creams. The fact that the Santa Monica plant dispensed 12,000 of these a day suggests the scale on which this vast plant operated. As Kevin Starr has written:

> Gigantic plants such as the Douglas plant in Santa Monica . . . were
> cities unto themselves, incorporating the full spectrum of urban
> functions—fire, police (with 162 officers, Douglas had the sixth

largest police department in California), transportation, branch city halls, lending libraries, voting booths.[82]

Douglas also offered entertainment and dances during lunch hour (whether "lunch" fell in the day, night, or wee hours of the morning) featuring music by the Douglas Welfare Band or other groups, and Hollywood stars made visits to buck up the plant's hardworking employees.

Wages were good at Douglas and the many extra services the company offered were attractive. However, wartime Santa Monica, and Los Angeles as well, suffered from an acute labor shortage. Stepped up war production and the fact that many able-bodied men were away in the armed services meant there were simply more jobs than people to fill them. Even greatly increased migration into the Los Angeles area by Americans looking for work during the war did not meet the need for workers. As a result, by January of 1942 Douglas, though formerly quite resistant, opened its doors to women workers who within months made up one third of the plant's workforce. Seeing the critical importance of female workers, federal officials helped organize day care centers for children and other services that made women's war work easier to integrate with family responsibilities. For many Santa Monica women life during the war was very different from life before (or after) because so many novel occupations were opened to them, their labor was much in demand, and they enjoyed much higher wages than they had been able to earn before. Not all of these gains would last when the fighting ended, but women's accomplishments did lay some groundwork for later struggles for equal rights.

Santa Monica's African Americans also saw their prospects improve thanks to war work at Douglas. Like women, blacks were excluded from aviation work prior to the war, and for a time after Pearl Harbor African Americans continued to be denied jobs. Lloyd Allen, a black resident of Santa Monica, was one who tried to get hired at Douglas early in the war but "couldn't get in" due to anti-black policies. He moved instead to Oakland where the Kaiser shipyard was already hiring African Americans. Indeed, in 1941 there were only four blacks employed in aviation in all of Southern California, not only because of company policies but also because the AFL Machinists Union, the principal union in the industry, explicitly barred blacks from joining. However, the acute need for workers inspired the federal government to enact anti-discriminatory hiring rules, which made Douglas and the unions more flexible, and African Americans started getting jobs. By the summer of 1942, for example, Joseph W. Spaulding, a young African American whose family had scraped by in Depression-era Santa Monica, was hired at Douglas the day after his graduation from Santa Monica High School.

To be sure, racial discrimination continued throughout the war. *Fortune* magazine's March 1943 issue reported "almost universal prejudice against the Negro" in Los Angeles defense plants, and black men and women were often relegated to the worst jobs.[83] Still, the wages were better than in other fields. Equally important, black participation in war production, as well as service in the military, helped pave the way for changes in the decades after the war. As one African-American employee at Douglas remembered:

> They didn't mix the white and black in the war. But now it gives you a kind of independence because they felt that we gone off and fought, we should be equal. Everything started openin' up for us. We got a chance to go places we had never been able to go before.[84]

The war was important for another reason as well, as it substantially increased the size of the city's African-American population. Once blacks started getting jobs in Los Angeles defense plants, they streamed into Southern California. By the summer of 1943 an estimated 10,000 to 12,000 were arriving each month in Los Angeles, many from rural towns in the South, and through the 1940s the county's black population tripled. Santa Monica's African-American population swelled as well. By one estimate there were about 500 blacks in Santa Monica before the war and by 1960 over 4,000 blacks called Santa Monica home, a number of whom had migrated during the war. This larger community, armed with wartime experience, would be increasingly vocal and organized in working for civil rights and equality once the fighting ended.

The experience of Mexican Americans during the war often paralleled that of African Americans. They too were subject to discriminatory hiring policies and hostility. (The famous Zoot Suit riots in which hundreds of off-duty servicemen attacked Hispanic youths occurred in nearby Los Angeles in 1943). But like African Americans, they made strides that lasted into the post-war period.

No matter what their race or sex, all the workers at Douglas in Santa Monica made a tremendous contribution to the war effort and Santa Monicans were justifiably proud of their important role. During the war 29,385 planes were produced by Douglas at all its plants, including models that played a pivotal role in America's victory. Among other models, Douglas made the Havoc, Dauntless, and Invader fighters as well as the famous C-47 Skytrain—a redesign of the DC-3—used to carry troops and cargo as well as drop paratroopers into enemy territory. In 1944, local newspaper editor Charles Warren boasted that, "Hardly a day passes that Donald Douglas does not receive some report on the part his planes are playing in the war effort."[85] This pride was well-founded. No less a figure than General Dwight Eisenhower would later declare that the C-47 was one of the four key weapons responsible for helping win the war (the bazooka, the Jeep, and the atom bomb were the other three).

With Douglas a beehive of activity, life during wartime in Santa Monica was transformed in many ways, and not always for the good. War production at Douglas provoked a large influx of newcomers to the city, helping to make the Los Angeles area the nation's fastest growing region. In addition, military operations in and around Santa Monica flooded the city with servicemen and women on and off duty. For one thing, Los Angeles served as a sort of funnel for thousands of soldiers and sailors on their way to fight in the Pacific theatre. Meanwhile military posts near Santa Monica, such as the Inglewood Air Force installation, brought many more armed services personnel into the area. In the four years between 1940 and 1944, Santa Monica went from 53,200 inhabitants to 65,000, a 22 percent increase. Population growth was not necessarily bad in itself, it was just that Santa Monica didn't have, and because of the war couldn't get, the resources or personnel to cope with the needs of so many newcomers.

One consequence of both civilian and military population growth was a critical housing shortage. Despite thousands of newcomers, only 203 new dwelling units were added to the city's housing stock from 1943 to 1944. The following year only 189 new units were constructed. This total would have been insufficient to house even normal population growth, much less the throngs now settling in the city. But with building materials unavailable and construction workers either in the armed services or working in vital war production, residents had to make do. Tight quarters, like rationing of food, clothing, and gas, were simply facts of life in wartime Santa Monica that would not be addressed until after the war.

The city's burgeoning population also put a serious strain on services. Schools and hospitals were overcrowded, and the fire and police departments were pushed to the limit, hampered by the loss of officers to the military. With gas and tire rationing in effect and many thousands of workers needing to get to Douglas day and night, the area's public transportation systems labored to meet the challenge. Already decrepit by the early 1940s, the Pacific Electric interurban trains hobbled through the war crammed with uncomfortable commuters, supplemented by the system's red buses. Santa Monica's own Big Blue Bus system (founded in 1928) added around-the-clock service to the Douglas plant, but was still pushed to capacity. Those who did use their cars created traffic bottlenecks, especially in the streets leading to the Douglas plant. The area's sewage system was so overwhelmed with wastewater that raw sewage was routinely dumped into Santa Monica Bay, leading to beach closures due to what a state board of health official called "massive, gross contamination."[86] Physicians in and around Santa Monica noted an increase in intestinal illnesses in those who dared to swim in the bay's fouled waters.

Despite these stresses there was still room for fun in Santa Monica, even during the war. But like so many other aspects of life, leisure in the city took on a unique quality, fueled by the hectic pace of life, the mixing of civilian and military people, and wartime restrictions. Some leisure activities were necessarily curtailed. The La Monica Ballroom, used as a roller rink during the Depression, was now converted and used as a bivouac for troops charged with protecting the coast. Meanwhile, none of the pleasure boats tied up in the harbor were allowed to operate during the war, though fishing boats still went out. Blackouts also put a damper on night life, forcing Santa Monica's amusement piers to restrict operations.

Mostly, however, Santa Monica's leisure industry, a fixture from the city's earliest days, adapted quite successfully to the exigencies of war. This was possible, in part, because Santa Monica found an important new buyer for its leisure services—the military. The armed forces appreciated the city's climate and facilities as well as its location on the Pacific, where much of the war was being fought. Indeed, Santa Monica played host to thousands upon thousands of off-duty military personnel during World War II, helping them recover from combat and enjoy some rest before new missions, in several of Santa Monica's beach clubs and hotels taken over by the military for that purpose. The Army Air Corps used the Miramar Hotel as a redistribution center for officers and soldiers returning from overseas duty. Aerial combat veterans were housed at the Casa del Mar and Edgewater clubs, as well as in the Shangri-La and Ocean Palms apartments for fifteen-day rest and relaxation breaks. Together, commandeered hotels and beach clubs hosted up to 2,000 off-duty military persons at a time. The armed forces also ran camps in Santa Monica that allowed thousands of soldiers short furloughs by the sea as a break from hard training at California's many desert or mountain military installations.

Santa Monica also provided many activities that worked around wartime restrictions but still offered diversion, not only for off-duty military men and women but also for defense workers coming off long shifts at Douglas and ordinary residents looking to forget their worries for awhile. Although Santa Monica's amusement piers did close during blackouts, they were open during the day and continued to welcome crowds using "dim out" procedures in which pier lights were shielded to reduce their visibility to the enemy. Ocean Park's piers were particularly popular, and the Lick Pier's Aragon Ballroom was renowned for its dances, attended by both servicemen and locals alike. Indeed, the "swing shift" dances, held on various beach piers between 12:30 a.m. and 6:00 a.m. to accommodate the odd hours of defense workers, were a little too popular as Santa Monica police found themselves repeatedly coping with large, unruly crowds. Other attractions switched to a twenty-four-hour-a-day schedule. Movies were popular and venues like the Aero Theatre on Montana Avenue, built by Donald Douglas in 1939, operated day and night. Bowling alleys also welcomed patrons at all hours. Despite wartime food rationing, restaurants also continued to operate, even if high standards were sometimes compromised. Occasionally, it seems, adapting to the exigencies of wartime went a little too far. Historian Arthur Verge tells this story:

> In Santa Monica, a popular hamburger restaurant that advertised itself as serving the biggest hamburgers in "the West" was shut down by authorities for false advertising after it was discovered that the thickly smothered "hamburgers" were actually thickly disguised horseburgers.[87]

Meanwhile the beach was, as ever, a magnet for people looking to relax and unwind. To protect those wishing to frolic in the surf, Santa Monica employed a largely female corps of lifeguards during World War II since most of the city's male guards had been called away. At Muscle Beach many of the regulars who had made the place popular during the Depression were absent due to war jobs or military service. Still, some returned when they could and new athletes began to work out there. They were joined by off-duty servicemen who used the beach nearby to do calisthenics. These attractions drew plenty of spectators and Muscle Beach remained popular throughout the war. Indeed for many thousands of people coming through Santa Monica, many of whom had never before been to Southern California, the beautiful bodies and the healthful, outdoor lifestyle on display there would provide a lasting memory once the war was over.

Oddly, in this time of dreadful world war, there was a lot of enjoyment to be found in Santa Monica. Yet the war could never really be pushed out of people's minds when almost everyone had friends or loved ones serving in combat zones. To be sure, the experience of war for Santa Monicans was also one of anguish and loss. Approximately 10,000 men and women from the Santa Monica Bay district served in the armed forces during World War II. Almost 500 of these were killed, and many more wounded. An anecdote about Principal Barnum of Santa Monica High School suggests the human toll of these figures. Bob Crawford, a math instructor at Santa Monica High School, recalled seeing Barnum each morning as he paced slowly back and forth in the school's outdoor amphitheatre. Periodically Barnum would stop at the school's memorial wall and stare at each of the names of the fallen inscribed there, and then resume his slow walk, only to return to the names again a few minutes later. Crawford observed Barnum repeat this ritual each morning and believed that the principal's failing health, leading to his death a few months later, was caused by the emotional stress of the war. Barnum's grief was but one example of what many Santa Monicans endured.

World War II ended on September 2, 1945, and right away much of the anguish, excitement, and mad rush to build airplanes subsided too. But the war left an indelible mark on Santa Monica. In a few short years the city had gained thousands of new residents and acquired a substantial industrial base. No longer on the periphery, it was now thoroughly integrated both into the regional and national economy. Leisure and tourism still had their place, but defense work had become a key pillar of the city's livelihood. The war wrought changes in Santa Monica's people as well. One ethnic group—the Japanese—had been expelled from the city, destroying a peaceful and productive community. But African Americans, Hispanics, and female Santa Monicans had an opposite experience—the war provided opportunities that would add energy to the fight for civil rights and equality after the war. And everyone who stayed in Santa Monica during the war had extraordinary experiences—from air raids, to long shifts at Douglas, to midnight dances, to painful goodbyes. The war years compressed a lot of living into a short time. Now, with the trauma of the Depression replaced by prosperity and the stress of war fading into memory, Santa Monica would set off on a path of feverish development that would continue to reshape the city in the post-war years.

Chapter Nine

CHANGE AND CONTROVERSY

AT MID-CENTURY

Just as the start of World War II transformed Santa Monica almost overnight, the end of the war meant a whole new set of changes as war production tapered off, military personnel returned from overseas, and civilian life resumed a calmer pace. However, life in Santa Monica did not return to "normal" in the late 1940s. Instead, these years were spent just trying to catch up to the transformations of the war years in everything from housing to civil rights to city government. Once the pressing needs created by the war had been addressed, the city then entered into a period of wholesale development in the 1950s, 1960s, and early 1970s as neighborhoods were razed and refashioned, Interstate 10 (the Santa Monica Freeway) cut through town, and city officials aired audacious proposals to remake the coastline. In these years Santa Monica as we know it today came into being. But this era did more than just reshape the physical environment. The unrestrained boldness of development in mid-century would eventually provoke a debate—played out most vividly in politics—about what the city should be. That debate continues to rage to this day.

Like Americans everywhere, Santa Monicans greeted the end of World War II with joyous celebration. However, jubilation was soon pushed aside as residents coped with the swing back to ordinary life. Housing shortages were one pressing problem no one could ignore. Already during the war newcomers seeking work at Douglas Aircraft had taken up residence in garages, guest houses, and spare rooms throughout the city, often with little attention to building codes or safety regulations. (One large home on Georgina Avenue, for example, had been carved into no less than twenty-six apartments and rented rooms.) Now, with the war over, a flood of returning service personnel, many of whom had been sent to Santa Monica for rest and relaxation during the war and liked it enough to settle permanently, added to the crisis. In early 1946, R.W. Haines, director of the local Veterans Information Center declared, "People are becoming desperate. We have 500 applications a month for housing that we are unable to meet." A Red Cross spokeswoman agreed, "The situation is tragic." The *Outlook* even reported on a plan to conduct "a house to house survey to determine to what extent the hoarding of unused living space was robbing service men of a chance to find a home."[88] Unfortunately, there were no fast solutions to crowding in Santa Monica, especially since building materials were in short supply after the war. It was only through the late 1940s, as new housing was steadily built, that relief finally came. A total of 5,196 new housing units added in Santa Monica between 1945 and 1949 brought much of the crunch to an end.

The shift to peacetime created stress at Douglas Aircraft as well. The factory that had beaten efficiency records cranking out aircraft twenty-four hours a day now downshifted as demand for military planes slackened and materials were in short supply. In the immediate post-war period, workers were laid off and the company entered a slump. Luckily for Douglas and the city's many aviation industry workers, there was a big market for commercial aircraft after the war as air travel became a major means of transportation both in the United States and abroad. Only about a year after the war's end in late 1946, Douglas delivered its first DC-6s to United Airlines and American Airlines. The DC-8 jetliner, which came into production during the 1950s, kept Douglas at the forefront of the industry. Thus, despite the immediate postwar downturn, Douglas remained the city's largest employer through the late 1940s and 1950s. And even after Douglas Aircraft merged with McDonnell in 1967 to become McDonnell-Douglas, the company remained an important force in the city until it closed operations in Santa Monica in 1975.

The end of the war was a time of transition for the city's exiled Japanese Americans as well. When Japanese exclusion from the West Coast was lifted in January of 1945, these former residents were at last freed from the internment camps where they had spent the war. However, while some of the city's former residents did return to Santa Monica, others, painfully aware of the humiliation they had suffered here, preferred to relocate to the Midwest or East Coast. For those who did return, their top priorities were reuniting with loved ones, reclaiming property, looking for jobs, and trying (like so many others) to secure housing. Unlike the shabby treatment they received during the war, Japanese Americans were generally welcomed back to Santa Monica. As historian Dana Blakemore stated, Santa Monica was "highly tolerant" of these returnees and was, in fact, commended by state officials for its "ideal viewpoint toward returnees" that included a pledge to protect their legal rights.[89] Still, even under these relatively favorable conditions, Japanese Americans faced a daunting task in trying to resume lives so abruptly interrupted. The Japanese-American community would never return to its pre-war vibrancy. The fact that some Santa Monicans—including both realtors and property owners—held on to old prejudices and refused to sell property to Asians well into the 1950s did not help.

Amidst these problems and stresses, Santa Monicans put their energy into projects long postponed because of the war. Revamping city government was one high priority. The demands of war, particularly the need to provide services for so many newcomers, had severely overtaxed local government and by the time peace was restored the city was near bankruptcy. Part of the problem was the city's outmoded form of government in which three equally powerful commissioners ran the city without help from professionally-trained managers. Aware that Santa Monica had become too large and complex for this sort of leadership, Santa Monicans agreed in December of 1945 to establish a board charged with rewriting the city's charter. By 1946 voters approved a new charter by a landslide of 14,206 to 6,161. The new charter promised to improve city governance by specifying a seven-member city council elected by the people, supplemented by a hired city manager appointed by the council. Under this new system—which is still in use today—the council's job was to set policy while the manager was charged with directing city staff and administration and seeing to the day-to-day running of city affairs. Implemented in 1947, the council-manager form of government quickly yielded improvements. The first city manager, Randall Dorton, who served until 1959, streamlined the city's administration, helped return the city to a sound financial footing and, to quote the *Outlook*, "started running things on a businesslike, rather than political basis."[90]

There was catching up to do in other areas as well. The years immediately after World War II saw an expansion of Santa Monica's business district as new shops opened catering to consumers eager to spend their money on items that had been unattainable during the Depression or unavailable during the war. Henshey's department store, a local institution that opened at Fourth Street and Santa Monica Boulevard in 1925, was now joined by national chains. Sears opened its distinctively post-war Modern building at its present location on Colorado between Third and Fourth Streets in July of 1947. Even with forty police officers on hand to manage the crowds, some 2,200 shoppers jammed the store in the first ten minutes eager to satisfy pent-up needs. J.C. Penney opened its doors on the corner of Third and Wilshire in 1949, attracting shoppers to the area and encouraging the opening of many new retail businesses on that block. Anchored by these stores, the downtown business district would thrive until around the mid-1950s.

Meanwhile, the leisure industry that had adapted so well during the war now returned to serving civilians. Some of the beach clubs and many hotels, such as the Miramar, which had been taken over by the military during the war, reopened to welcome their traditional well-heeled clientele. Sports enthusiasts—always plentiful in Santa Monica—organized some of Southern California's first beach volleyball tournaments starting in 1948. And Muscle Beach continued to attract large audiences who marveled at the sculpted bodies on display there. The Miss Muscle Beach and Mr. Muscle Beach contests that began in 1947 offered an added attraction to an already alluring scene. (Indeed Muscle Beach remained hugely popular right up until 1958, when city officials abruptly shut it down in response to a sex scandal involving rape charges against several Muscle Beach bodybuilders.) At night the city's piers hopped with the sounds of Spade Cooley and his orchestra at the La Monica Ballroom, and Lawrence Welk and his "Champagne" musicians at the Aragon Ballroom on Lick Pier in Ocean Park. Cooley's shows, featuring "Western swing" music, were broadcast on local television on Saturday nights and attracted enthusiastic crowds from 1946 until 1954. Lawrence Welk achieved even greater fame when his performances were broadcast first locally on KTLA and then nationally for sixteen years on the ABC network.

For some Santa Monicans, especially the city's African Americans, such frivolity would take a backseat to more important work—the effort to hold onto and advance gains achieved during the war. Blacks in Santa Monica had been involved in working towards improved economic opportunities and greater civil rights before the war. A local chapter of the NAACP had formed as early as 1918. Before World War II some local blacks, including Alfred T. Quinn (who would later become the first black teacher hired in Santa Monica and an important leader of the African-American community), organized actions challenging local restaurants, such as Henn's Drive-In, that refused to serve them. By 1940, Santa Monica blacks also had a newspaper, *The Bay Cities Informer*, which proclaimed its dedication to "the advancement and welfare of our people and our community" and ran stories calling for better city services for the black and ethnic Pico neighborhood, as well as calls for self-improvement. Around 1944 another newspaper, *The Plaindealer*, helped publicize issues of interest to local blacks.

During the war the struggle continued as blacks in Los Angeles and Santa Monica strove for improved opportunities in war industry. They also took direct action to reduce the de facto segregation that prevailed in many Santa Monica establishments. Their unsung efforts for justice made a difference. For example, towards the end of the war an African American named John Rucker Jr. took his date to the Wilshire Theatre and deliberately sat down in the section reserved for whites. He was soon told by theatre managers that he could not remain there. When he refused to move, saying he had paid his money and would stay put, the police were called to arrest him. In the end Rucker took the Wilshire Theatre to court with the support of the NAACP and won the case. The theatre was not only fined but also informed that it would be fined even more for any other similar instances. Rucker then patronized the other movie houses in Santa Monica, breaking down segregation based on the court's judgment wherever he went.

Now with the war over, Santa Monica blacks worked to be part of the economic prosperity other Americans were starting to enjoy. In one case, shortly after the new Sears store opened, a black veteran named George Whittaker applied for a sales job there. But Sears refused to hire any blacks, veterans or not. Soon the NAACP and local blacks worked together to form picket lines around the store. Lloyd Allen, a longtime Santa Monican who was there, remembers that about 250 people picketed, both black and white. Although Sears proved remarkably resistant to the picketers' demands, eventually one black was hired as a stock clerk, paving the way for others later. Allen also remembered efforts to open up jobs beyond janitorial work at companies like General Telephone (GTE) and Safeway grocery stores. GTE eventually agreed to hire one black and a very highly qualified woman was selected. Her excellent performance led to five more hires, which in time led to even more jobs. Blacks were not paid the same wages as whites at GTE, but they were making important inroads. Santa Monica's Safeway grocery store was another target for activists who, again, after meeting resistance succeeded in getting the company to employ one worker and later more. Opportunities to work for the city were slowly opening up as well, thanks to pressure from African Americans. There was still room for a great deal of improvement well into the 1960s and beyond but Santa Monica's blacks began to see some positive changes in the years after World War II. Under the leadership of men such as Reverend Welford P. Carter of Calvary Baptist Church and the venerable educator Dr. Quinn, the civil rights movement in Santa Monica would continue to gain strength and further advance the cause of Santa Monica's black community in the decades to come. That progress that had been made was undeniable when Nathaniel Trives became the city's first African-American mayor in 1975.

If the late 1940s were a time for catching up to the changes brought on by the war, the 1950s were a time when city leaders and residents moved forward to update and improve Santa Monica, and build even more homes and businesses. Newcomers continued to seek out Santa Monica. In its heyday in the 1950s many families took Route 66—America's favorite highway— to its endpoint in Santa Monica and stayed for good. Building continued apace as the city's population swelled from 71,500 in 1950 to more than 83,000 ten years later. In Santa Monica, as in Southern California generally during this prosperous period, development, the more the better, was the watchword.

In the prosperous 1950s, civic projects that had been impossible earlier became a priority for the city. A new Fairview branch library building on Ocean Park Boulevard and Twenty-first Street was built in 1956 and the groundbreaking on a new Montana branch facility at Montana Avenue and Seventeenth Street took place in 1959. The city also built new reservoirs to improve Santa Monica's water supply. To ameliorate some of the water pollution problems caused by the region's burgeoning population, Santa Monica, in conjunction with the city of Los Angeles and other neighboring districts, helped to construct the Hyperion water treatment plant in Marina del Rey. The plant was in operation by the early 1960s. It was also at this time that the Santa Monica Civic Center really began to take shape. A new city hall had been constructed during the Depression at 1685 Main Street. In 1956 a new county building and civic auditorium were added nearby, both of which still stand today on Main Street. The civic auditorium, which could accommodate several thousand and featured a floor adaptable to everything from sporting events to musical programs, was built to help attract conventions to Santa Monica, as well as house events of interest to locals. For several years in the 1960s it hosted such high profile events as the Academy Awards.

However, the expansion of the civic center necessarily required the destruction of a neighborhood that housed lower income residents. As far as the city was concerned, this was not necessarily a bad thing. Indeed, several of the city's annual reports during the 1950s highlighted the city's focused effort to sweep away "substandard" structures and require those that remained to meet city codes. Among the accomplishments listed in the city's 1951–1952 Annual Report, for example, was the fact that in the previous five years some 350 dilapidated dwellings were "eliminated . . . together with a considerable number of old sheds, rat-infested outbuildings, and other structures."[91] To be sure some of this was necessary for health and safety reasons and, in an era before historic preservation became a priority, razing old buildings was a sign of progress. Still, in the process some structures that today would be considered historically significant were inevitably destroyed.

Besides these changes to the city's built environment, Santa Monica officials also began to consider more elaborate urban renewal schemes in the 1950s. The Ocean Park area with its many old bungalows by the beach came under particular scrutiny. By the 1950s, Ocean Park was no longer the tourist's paradise it had once been. In the 1940s and 1950s, property values in the area dropped and the scores of small bungalows that had once been quaint seaside abodes were increasingly dilapidated, now housing a mix of racially diverse and elderly low-income residents. It all looked like an eyesore to city officials. In 1958 the city acted on this assessment, establishing a redevelopment district in Ocean Park and designating the twenty-five acres that stretched from Barnard and Neilson Ways to Ocean Park Boulevard and the city's southern limits "blighted." By 1960 the city developed a plan for the area that included two seventeen-story apartment buildings and space for other new structures as well. Working to make this plan a reality, the city then acquired the 259 separate parcels of land involved and destroyed the homes and buildings that stood on them. In all, 316 families, 502 individuals, and 212 businesses had to be relocated elsewhere. In theory these displaced persons were entitled to assistance from the redevelopment agency in finding affordable housing elsewhere, but in practice few did. One exception was a group of elderly poor who were accommodated in an apartment building on city-owned land in another location.

Once cleared, construction began on the first phase of redevelopment, Santa Monica Shores. These two apartment towers, located at Neilson Way, opened in 1966. Other plans for development on the land that included cooperative apartments, as well as twenty-two-story luxury apartments, were stymied, however, when Californians passed Proposition 20 in 1972, limiting coastal building. The end result was that at a cost of $14 million the city had eliminated a neighborhood and replaced it with 532 nice apartments. Although some Santa Monicans would certainly enjoy living in these beachside units, even Les Storrs, the city's planning and zoning director, acknowledged the downside:

> Subsequent to the building of Santa Monica Shores, considerable criticism was voiced, not only in Santa Monica but nationwide, on the ground that redevelopment tends to oust the poor from their homes and to build housing for the affluent on the same site.[92]

But whatever criticism was voiced, this would not be the last time lower-income Santa Monicans would be required to leave their homes because of the city's larger plans.

Meanwhile, private building was occurring throughout the city as old structures made way for new ones and lots in areas like Sunset Park (in the south-east quadrant of the city) were developed for the first time. In the years between 1955 and 1960 an average of 1,345 new dwelling units were constructed each year. Increasingly, these new living spaces were not single-family houses but apartment buildings. Santa Monica Shores was but an extreme example of a trend that was occurring throughout the city and that would change Santa Monica dramatically as it intensified through the 1960s and 1970s. Les Storrs has pointed to the city's zoning ordinances established in 1929 and revised in 1937 and 1948 as paving the way for apartment building construction in the mid-twentieth century. These regulations, along with the steady demand for housing, meant that by the 1960s only a small fraction of new building was in single-family homes. In the 1964–1965 fiscal year, for example, only nine new dwellings out of 1,243 were traditional houses, and in 1967–1968 only ten out of 1,414 were single-family homes. By 1974 fully four out of five Santa Monicans were apartment dwellers.

That Santa Monica's city officials generally favored development in the 1950s is not surprising. Real estate development had long been the lynchpin of prosperity in Southern California. Neither historic preservation nor environmentalism was part of the language of the day. Moreover, to Americans of the 1950s preoccupied with the Cold War and on the lookout for subversive "Reds" at home, any restraints on business or developers looked suspiciously like Communism. (Quite ironically, this shift from a town of modest bungalows and handsome houses to a city dominated by stucco apartment buildings would actually help bring on a shift to "radical" politics in Santa Monica later in the century when renters banded together to try to restrain the kind of freewheeling development that had built their apartments in the first place.)

As these physical changes were occurring, Santa Monica's economy was also under construction. Douglas Aircraft was the city's most important employer, but other companies rounded out the picture. Some, such as the Rand Corporation, were defense-related. Rand, a research-based nonprofit organization, was heavily involved in mid-century with the analysis of issues related to national security, and by the early 1950s was installed in a large building at 1700 Main Street housing hundreds of employees. (A new Rand building is under construction as of 2004.) Systems Development Corporation, a spin-off of Rand, was formed in 1956 and would grow to be another of the city's major firms, employing hundreds on defense-related projects. The *Outlook* reported that, "In 1962 Santa Monica had some 250 companies with emphasis on electronics, space and missile components, and research and development."[93] Santa Monica's Chamber of Commerce also worked to attract non-defense-related enterprises to the city. Paper Mate moved to the city in 1957 and became one of the city's largest employers, manufacturing pens at its plant on Twenty-sixth Street. Indeed, Santa Monica's industrial corridor, bounded roughly by Olympic Boulevard and Colorado Avenue (and now partially eroded by new office and apartment buildings), took shape in this era.

The city's leisure industry played less of a role in sustaining Santa Monica than it had in years past. Still, Santa Monica's beaches attracted many visitors, and entrepreneurs continued to look for ways to profit from tourism. One ambitious attempt to revitalize the amusement pier concept was Pacific Ocean Park, a nautical-themed amusement park designed to rival Anaheim's Disneyland. A $15-million venture, POP, as it came to be known, was built after CBS and the

Hollywood Turf Club acquired the lease on twenty-eight acres of beachfront property and the old Ocean Park Pier at the Venice border in 1956. When it opened in 1958, visitors flocked to see the corporate-sponsored attractions that included Coca-Cola's Neptune's Kingdom, featuring motorized sea creatures, a futuristic atomic model city underwritten by Westinghouse, a Flight to Mars ride reflecting the era's fixation on rockets and space aliens, and the Ocean Skyway, which suspended riders over the ocean in transparent bubbles for a trip to the end of the pier and back. POP also included more traditional rides with ocean themes, games and shooting galleries, a merry-go-round, and a funhouse. Unfortunately, while many young Santa Monicans found the park irresistible, POP was not the success its backers had hoped for and it closed its doors in 1967 to start a new life as a major safety hazard and eyesore until its remains were finally removed by the city in 1975. However, in its years of operation it carried on the tradition of leisure innovation in Santa Monica and contributed to the city's economy.

Overall, the mix of companies in Santa Monica in the 1950s and early 1960s meant that Santa Monica was a town with a significant blue-collar element (though there were plenty of white collar residents as well). Despite the fact that the city had worked to eliminate very poor housing, Santa Monica was still a place where families with a wide range of incomes could feel comfortable. However, the city's population would continue to grow—another 10,000 people moved to Santa Monica in the fifteen years after 1960 for a total population of 93,500 by 1975—and ambitious new development projects continued to be approved by city officials. Under these circumstances, gentrification was just around the corner.

Efforts to make the downtown area more upscale contributed to this trend. Santa Monicans today are well aware of the city's efforts to tinker with the downtown area in order to attract shoppers and tourists. What many do not know is that this has been an ongoing project for about fifty years. It started in the mid-1950s when city officials and local business leaders began to feel that the downtown shopping area, centered on Third Street, was "standing still." A consultant hired by the city to investigate the area concluded it was "not living up to its potential and if the situation was not corrected would lead to continued deterioration and decay."[94] Santa Monica's business people particularly feared that new shopping areas planned for Century City, Culver City, West Los Angeles, and the San Fernando Valley would draw business away from Santa Monica. They were right to be worried. A new kind of shopping experience was sweeping the Southland—the outdoor "mall"—in which specialty shops lined pleasantly landscaped outdoor promenades and cars were easily parked in adjacent parking garages. This kind of shopping haven was more attractive to consumers than vintage downtown areas where traffic was congested and parking scarce.

By 1963, the city had formulated a response: Santa Monica would join the trend and have an outdoor mall of its own with an easy-to-remember name—Santa Monica Mall. By November of 1965, Third Street from Wilshire to Broadway had been transformed into a pedestrian mall. Six new multi-story parking garages able to accommodate up to 2,500 cars were well on the way to completion nearby. Bandleader Lawrence Welk, a major commercial property owner in Santa Monica by this time, provided entertainment on opening day. In the years after the mall opened, Santa Monica's taxable sales figures were on the upswing, surpassing neighboring Los Angeles. For the moment at least Santa Monica's attractiveness to shoppers seemed assured.

Other new developments were also reshaping the downtown area around the same time. The staid old main library was torn down in 1965 to be replaced by a modern new building on Sixth Street near Santa Monica Boulevard (demolished in 2003 to make way for yet another new main library). Meanwhile, private developers pushed forward a bumper crop of new projects. The 1968–1969 fiscal year was particularly striking. The city's annual report proudly stated that Santa Monica's "progress" was marked "by an unusually large number of major developments for which plans were either announced or completed." These included the Wilshire West complex, which featured a twenty-two-story office tower at Wilshire Boulevard and Ocean Avenue to be occupied by GTE as its corporate headquarters. With Lawrence Welk as the principal stockholder, Wilshire West also included the "top quality" Champagne Towers apartments next door.[95]

The city added to the increasingly vertical look of the downtown area by building a nine-level parking structure on Second Street to help serve the Wilshire West buildings. New bank buildings included the Wells Fargo headquarters at Fourth and Arizona as well as City National Plaza at 606 Wilshire. The multi-story Holiday Inn at Colorado and Ocean and the Royal Inn Hotel across from the Civic Auditorium opened in 1967 and 1968 respectively, adding to the transformation of the city. More development planned for the early 1970s included two "Ocean Towers" apartment buildings approved in 1970 to be built at Ocean and San Vicente. Around 1971 the city also began toying with the idea of a new downtown regional shopping center across from Sears, which would eventually come to fruition in 1980 as the Frank Gehry-designed Santa Monica Place. Clearly development was dear to the hearts of city officials in the 1960s and early 1970s.

However, pockets of resentment towards the wholesale reshaping of the city were beginning to emerge, and the coming of the Interstate 10 freeway galvanized at least some Santa Monicans against the more destructive aspects of post-war development. The completion of the 10 Freeway to the coast was part of a plan by regional transportation officials to put all Southern Californians within four miles of a freeway. With the Southland's population widely dispersed, post-war transportation planners, having long since given up on the idea of extensive public transportation, looked to freeways as the answer to the region's traffic problems. But, in Santa Monica at least, the freeway had wide-ranging effects that went far beyond just improving transportation.

For a time the final endpoint of Interstate 10 was up for debate, but due to the advocacy of Robert E. McClure, a longtime editor of the *Outlook*, civic leader, member of the state highway commission, and Santa Monica booster, Santa Monica won out over other possible sites such as neighboring Venice. There were good reasons to want an eight-lane freeway running through the city. Business leaders in Santa Monica thought a major freeway with exits near the downtown area would be good for local merchants because it would bring the "entire westerly portion of the Los Angeles metropolitan area within 20 minutes driving time from Santa Monica."[96] If Santa Monica were "freeway close," it would certainly encourage leisure visitors as well. And for those Santa Monicans who had reason to go to downtown Los Angeles—a daunting one and a half hour ordeal through 119 traffic lights via Wilshire Boulevard—a freeway had obvious appeal. Once it was decided that California freeways would be named for their endpoints, some felt the publicity the city would receive was valuable. As McClure remarked, "The best thing for Santa Monica was to have this place designated as the western terminal for the national highway system. That meant the name Santa Monica would be on all highway signs leading to the coast."[97] For many in Santa Monica, Interstate 10, even if it sliced directly through the city, was a sign of progress, convenience, and future prosperity.

Work was begun on the freeway in the late 1950s, but the 16.2 mile stretch from the Santa Ana Freeway to the coast was a massive undertaking that took time. Property owners in the freeway's path had to be bought out, thousands of homes and commercial structures had to be demolished, and mountains of land had to be rearranged before the roadway could be laid. By December 1964, the Sawtelle to Bundy segment had been completed and work commenced in earnest in Santa Monica. In January of 1966, Interstate 10 finally reached the tunnel (now the Robert E. McClure Tunnel) to Pacific Coast Highway and the newly dubbed "Santa Monica Freeway" officially began its life as a major regional artery and the last leg of an interstate highway that ran over 2,500 miles, all the way from Jacksonville, Florida. Right away, of course, the freeway was popular with motorists. In its first year the Santa Monica Freeway carried an average of 95,000 cars a day at a point just west of the San Diego Freeway. Some 32,000 cars a day used the freeway just east of the McClure Tunnel and each year would bring more users. As far as speeding up the flow of traffic was concerned, there is little doubt that the Santa Monica Freeway was a success.

However, moving traffic through the city was only one result of the coming of the freeway. In many different ways the freeway altered patterns of life in Santa Monica. The most immediate and dramatic effect was on Santa Monica's ethnic minorities. In a decision that has both been defended as economically sensible and decried as racist, city officials elected to route the freeway directly through the heart of the city's ethnic neighborhood. In the process, the area that African Americans knew as the Pico Quarter or Pico Neighorhood, Hispanic residents knew as *La Veinte*, and Japanese-Americans also called home, was eviscerated by the freeway.

We have already seen how in the post-war period, Santa Monica's African-American community was working towards greater civil rights and improved economic opportunities. By the mid-1960s important strides had been made and the black neighborhood, though modest, was populated by many homeowners, black-owned businesses, and community groups. The freeway pulled the rug out from under all this as African-American families were forced to sell their property to make way for the new road. Because they lived in a minority neighborhood, property values were lower than elsewhere, and many blacks found that what they got for their homes was not enough to buy elsewhere in Santa Monica, especially when the neighborhoods north of Wilshire and south of Pico were still effectively closed to blacks.

The result was that, as black community leader Blanche Carter stated, "We lost many people who had to sell their homes during that time. It came down the middle of our community and deprived a lot of people of their homes." Important community institutions were also weakened. The city's African Methodist Episcopal Church, for example, saw its membership dwindle from 500 to only 250 after the freeway was built. Many African Americans, some of whom were native Santa Monicans, moved to neighboring Venice or Los Angeles and retained ties to Santa Monica, returning for church or social events, but the community would never be the same.

It was not that African Americans didn't protest the route. On the contrary, the *Outlook* reported that the Reverend Welford Carter of Calvary Baptist Church and other black community leaders voiced their objections, "but they just couldn't persuade planners to move the route of the freeway."[98] Some black residents like Frank Richardson, who managed a smoke shop at Olympic and Seventeenth, were philosophical. "The freeway" he said, "was progress. However, it did work hardships on people." Others, such as one African American quoted in the *Outlook* in 1964 stated, "Santa Monica wants to make this a place for rich whites. They want to make it a resort town. They are trying to move the Negroes and Mexicans out of here."[99] Not surprisingly, a sense of bitterness at the destruction wrought by the freeway still lingers today among some local African Americans.

The city's Mexican-American residents also suffered from the coming of the freeway. A large percentage of the city's Hispanic families had long lived in the area between Fourteenth and Twentieth from Olympic to Pico Boulevards. Freeway construction uprooted many of these households and squeezed the community into a smaller area. As with blacks, many long-time Mexican-American residents, no longer able to afford the city, were obliged to relocate to West Los Angeles, Culver City, and elsewhere. Although in the years between 1960 and 1970 the city's Spanish-surname population actually rose from 5,145 to 10,668 because of new immigration from Mexico, the city's established Hispanic community was, in the words of Marquez family descendant Forrest Freed, "decimated by the freeway." Freed, like many blacks, saw the city's choice of route for the freeway as "a prejudicial move."[100]

The freeway affected the city's Japanese Americans as well. Already evicted once from their homes during World War II, some of those who had returned to Santa Monica found themselves thrown out of their homes again by Interstate 10. All too often they too were unable to find new homes in Santa Monica. Historian Dana Blakemore noted that, "Several minority community leaders accused the city's planning commission of discriminating against central corridor residents on account of their ethnicity and lack of political and economic power," but their complaints went largely unheard.[101] Whatever the intentions of city decision-makers, the effect of building the freeway through Santa Monica's densest minority area effectively counteracted several decades of civil-rights improvements. Lives and businesses that had been painstakingly built up were disbanded and long-time residents were pushed out of the city altogether. Moreover, by agreeing to destroy a large pocket of affordable housing in the city, officials reduced the economic diversity of the city and thereby discouraged minorities from seeking homes in Santa Monica in the future.

Aside from these dramatic effects, the new freeway influenced how life was lived in Santa Monica in more subtle ways. From a physical point of view, even areas distant from the freeway felt its effects as once quiet residential streets were reconfigured to serve as tributaries to the new river of traffic flowing through town. Around 1966, for example, city crews widened Twenty-sixth Street in order to make possible "a free flow of traffic from the northerly city limits to the Santa Monica Freeway."[102] Other neighborhoods saw similar changes as the city reoriented itself to Interstate 10.

The local economy, which business leaders hoped would be affected positively by the freeway, also underwent changes, some not anticipated. For one thing the city's merchants soon learned that, "A freeway is a two-way street . . . in addition to bringing customers to the Santa Monica central business district, the freeway also takes money into other shopping centers." A decade after the freeway was completed, Sam Porter, a Chamber of Commerce official, also noted that not much new manufacturing had come to Santa Monica as a result of the freeway. However, Porter remarked, "What the freeway did was make it more likely that big companies would have their offices here." It is not surprising then that the late 1960s and early 1970s saw a rash of new office building in Santa Monica.

If office space was at a new premium, residential real estate in the city suddenly became a lot more attractive as well. As local bank president Aubrey Austin remarked, the freeway made "an attractive place more accessible to more people." The result was soaring land prices, increased demolition of old homes, more apartment buildings springing up in their places, and higher rents as Santa Monica became more of a suburb for the greater Los Angeles area and less a place where people both lived and worked. According to the Chamber of Commerce's Sam Porter, "The availability of land became zilch. . . . You had to tear down two single-family homes to build one 20-unit apartment."[103] These forces, combined with the whittling away of low-income housing that occurred in the late 1940s, 1950s, and early 1960s, meant that gentrification was now well underway in Santa Monica.

Overall, the freeway had huge effects on Santa Monica, and not all of them were good. Yet, with the exception of the city's minorities, who were directly hurt by the project, the freeway was welcomed. However, the 1960s were awash in new ideas, many of which ran counter to the business-as-usual development ethos of mid-century. As the impact of the freeway was being felt and these new ways of thinking— including elements of anti-business feeling, an interest in preserving a "human-scale" lifestyle, and a respect for the environment—started coming into focus, the city and developers would find it increasingly difficult to forge ahead in Santa Monica. Indeed, when the city tried to meddle with the coastline—something precious to all Santa Monicans—anti-development sentiment coalesced into a coherent movement that could not be ignored.

By the late 1960s, Santa Monica's seaside leisure operations had been in decline for some time. The breakwater and harbor projects, built in the 1930s with the hope of attracting well-to-do boaters, never really panned out, yet the city continued to be saddled with large maintenance costs. Ocean Park's amusement pier was revitalized, at least temporarily, by Pacific Ocean Park, but what is known today as the Santa Monica Pier was languishing. (For simplicity I refer to "the pier," but Santa Monica Pier is actually two side-by-side piers: the old Municipal Pier on the north and the Santa Monica Pleasure Pier on the south. The Santa Monica Pleasure Pier was also known as the Looff Pier and, in the 1960s, as the Newcomb Pier.) Though the pier did feature restaurants, snack bars, the carousel, arcade games, and plenty of room for fishermen, its long-term future was in doubt, especially since the owner of the Newcomb portion, Enid Newcomb Winslow, was obligated to demolish it when her contract with the city expired in 1973. Moreover, parts of the pier were falling to pieces, including the once-glittering La Monica Ballroom, which had to be torn down in 1962 due to a dangerously sagging roof. Given these circumstances, it is not surprising that Santa Monica officials were thinking hard about how best to manage and develop the city's coastline and seaside amenities. Bold action, it seemed, was needed.

Beginning in 1959, when the state decided to transform Pacific Coast Highway (California Highway 1) into a major freeway as part of a master plan to upgrade California's roads, the issue of what the coast should look like started coming to a head. Over the course of the next twelve years, as the state, the federal government, and Santa Monica's city officials studied the question of what route such a major highway would take through the city, three options emerged, each with implications for the quality of life in Santa Monica. One proposal involved an offshore causeway, supported by a series of islands, that would run over the water alongside Santa Monica before turning inland around Topanga—essentially a freeway on the bay. A second option was a freeway along the beach requiring special engineering of the beach itself. The third possibility was a route through Pacific Palisades.

The city was certainly in favor of a new freeway to carry heavy coastal traffic. Of the possibilities under consideration the city endorsed the causeway plan as the best solution. Indeed, after the U.S. Army Corps of Engineers declared such a causeway technically feasible in 1963, the city council was so eager to advance the project that it allocated $50,000, in part to pay an engineering firm for detailed plans. As described by historian Jeffrey Stanton, the plans that were drawn up:

> featured a causeway that extended a mile out to sea on a series of
> man-made islands. The route, which enclosed 3,200 acres . . . ran

from the Santa Monica Pier to just north of Topanga Canyon. The islands would be 65% residential with the remainder devoted to schools, churches and parks. The project, which would need 200 million cubic yards of fill at a cost of $90 million, would be the world's largest earth moving project.[104]

Enthusiasts of the causeway scheme, such as Robert E. McClure (who had been so instrumental in bringing the 10 Freeway through Santa Monica), claimed that such a causeway would be both "attractive and inoffensive."[105]

That the city was willing to back such a plan certainly speaks volumes about official confidence in the ability to remake the natural environment. To say that if such a causeway had actually been built would have dramatically altered the look and feel of Santa Monica is an understatement. Not to mention that the city seemed to have learned so little from its much more modest, but still unsatisfactory and expensive, experience with the harbor and breakwater. In retrospect it seems quite fortunate that Los Angeles, which was also a party to these negotiations, backed away from the causeway idea by 1968. Indeed, by 1971 Santa Monica officials, the Chamber of Commerce, and pro-development forces (which also favored an enlarged road in whatever form it might take) found that Santa Monicans too were refusing to support the freeway at all, whether it involved a causeway or not. The *Outlook* later credited a group called Santa Monica Bay Area Freeway Citizens Committee, rising environmental consciousness, and a last-minute change of heart by the city council with helping to kill the whole plan for a coastal freeway in Santa Monica. In the end, the state legislature simply deleted the Santa Monica to Ventura County portion of the proposed freeway from the state's master highway plan.

However, city officials, particularly ambitious city manager Perry Scott, were apparently not chastened by growing resistance to coastline development. Even as the freeway issue was winding down, Scott devised a plan in conjunction with the Mutual Development Company for a twenty-five-acre island to be built just offshore from the city. Formally presented to the city council in 1972, the plan would have required sweeping away the existing piers (today's Santa Monica Pier) and would have featured restaurants, shops, a sports pavilion, a boat dock, a fishing lagoon, and, to cap it all off, a twenty-nine-story, 1,500-room hotel. Despite the fact that voters had already declined to fund a much smaller island plan proposed by Scott in 1967, the city council scheduled a public hearing and seemed ready to pursue "Santa Monica Island."

The public hearing revealed some deep animosity to the island plan among Santa Monicans, as well as resistance from organizations like the Los Angeles chapter of the Sierra Club. Opponents feared not only significant damage to the coastal ecosystem, but also the blighted views caused by the proposed hotel. Nonetheless, the city council voted 6–0 in favor of the island. Soon a "Save the Santa Monica Bay Committee" formed to try to prevent the island from being built, and public outcry reached a fever pitch. By January of 1973, when another hearing on the island plan was held, more than a thousand people showed up. Most attended to express their dislike for the plan. Forced by public pressure to back down, the city council finally voted 4–2 to abandon the island plan.

But the city council jumped out of the frying pan and into the fire when, at the same meeting, its members resolved to tear down both the Municipal and Newcomb portions of the pier. As Mayor Anthony Dituri expressed it, "The pier is a tired, old and dingy thing and the economics of fixing it up are not worth it."[106] Many, however, strongly disagreed. Energized by the fight against Santa Monica Island, a vocal opposition soon formed consisting of both pier businesspeople and ordinary residents. Fed up with a city council and city manager who seemed all too ready to throw away the city's heritage and charm, Santa Monicans rallied around the pier. The city council relented in February 1973 and agreed to save the Municipal portion of the pier, but in April of 1973 Santa Monicans still ousted all three of the incumbent councilmen up for re-election, each of whom had been in favor of tearing down the pier. In their places voters elected advocates of more tightly controlled coastal development. To further make their point, Santa Monicans passed an initiative, by a stunning 78 percent, making voter approval a requirement for any future major development in Santa Monica Bay.

Under Mayor Clo Hoover, the new city council fired pro-development city manager Perry Scott immediately. Soon after, it voted to save the Newcomb section of the pier. And by 1974 the city agreed to purchase that part of the pier and the land at its entrance, thereby assuring city control of Santa Monica Pier into the future. As World War II receded into memory, and the social and political upheavals of the 1960s and 1970s took center stage, a new era was clearly beginning as Santa Monicans sought to redefine what the city should be. The time of totally unbridled development was waning, giving way to a new era of "radical" politics that would steer the city on a new course.

Chapter Ten

TO THE PRESENT

In the last thirty years, a great deal has happened in the 8.3 square miles that make up Santa Monica. Change has come in many forms, from the sudden physical transformation wrought by the Northridge Earthquake, to more subtle economic, social, and political developments. Yet while Santa Monica is certainly different now than it was a few decades ago, in some ways the city has remained true to its historical roots. To give just one example, tourism is still a mainstay of the local economy much as it was from Santa Monica's earliest days. This chapter offers an evaluation of Santa Monica's recent past, seen through the lens of history. In this brief review one story stands out as particularly important for understanding the city today—the tension between left-leaning politics and gentrification that has brought Santa Monica to a crossroads in the early twenty-first century.

Let's begin with the dramatic. Much of this history of Santa Monica has been concerned with human actions and their effects. It is sometimes easy to forget that nature has its own way of creating change in Southern California—earthquakes. From before the time when the first Spanish explorers mapped out the Los Angeles Basin to the present day, earthquakes have been a fact of life. Their power to devastate has been magnified as more and more people have flocked to Southern California, a fact that hit home in the wee hours of January 17, 1994. At that moment a powerful earthquake changed Santa Monica with a speed and brutality those who lived through it will not soon forget.

The quake, measuring 6.7 on the Richter scale, originated some distance from Santa Monica in Northridge, but the city was still remarkably hard hit. Residents awoke to the sounds and sights of buildings lurching, windows breaking, and belongings crashing to the ground, as some 1,500 buildings sustained damage and 2,300 housing units in Santa Monica were instantly rendered uninhabitable. In just a few minutes the Northridge Earthquake did an estimated $250 million dollars of damage in Santa Monica. Once the shaking stopped, residents found that the city's two hospitals, Santa Monica Hospital and St. John's Hospital, were both crippled by the quake, adding to the chaos and making help for the injured difficult to find. In neighboring Los Angeles, the quake did massive damage as well. Fifty-eight people lost their lives, thousands were injured, and 100,000 buildings were damaged.

Soon the entire region was designated a disaster area and help began to flow in. However, the fact that the Santa Monica Freeway collapsed in central Los Angeles, cutting off a vital artery in and out of Santa Monica, and that many businesses were badly damaged, hindered any return to normal life for quite some time. Because of the Northridge Earthquake, many structures in Santa Monica were demolished or entirely rebuilt. On the Santa Monica College campus, for example, the science and liberal arts buildings, as well as the library and parking structures, had to be replaced. Other buildings, such as the main library downtown, were eventually able to reopen but hobbled on with lingering damage. Even now, ten years after the earthquake, there are still structures in Santa Monica that have not yet been repaired.

The earthquake, of course, brought instant change to Santa Monica. Other transformations in the recent past, such as those involving the city's economy, have been subtler. A new industrial park was built in the 1970s near Stewart Street, but the importance of manufacturing in Santa Monica has steadily declined from its heyday in the mid-twentieth century. Douglas Aircraft, a major force in the local economy, left the city in 1975 and the lack of large open spaces for new industrial plants, as well as high real estate prices, have discouraged large manufacturing firms from locating here. However, Santa Monica's attractiveness as a place for offices, a trend that took off after Interstate 10 came to town, has continued to the present. In recent years several large office complexes have been built, including sizeable developments near Cloverfield Boulevard, particularly on Colorado Avenue. As offices take over space that once belonged to the city's industrial corridor, white-collar activities have supplanted manufacturing, both as a source of jobs and as a source of revenue for Santa Monica.

Entertainment firms are especially numerous among the businesses using office and commercial space in the city. Indeed, from its roots in Hollywood in the twentieth century, the entertainment industry has been slowly migrating west over time and Santa Monica has been a logical destination. While it is true that Metro-Goldwyn-Mayer moved out of its Santa Monica headquarters in 2003, taking 1,000 jobs with it, many other music, film, and television firms find Santa Monica convenient, from large companies like Universal Music and MTV, to scores of smaller firms providing goods and services to the entertainment industry.

The entertainment industry, moreover, plays a role in Santa Monica's economy beyond just renting offices here. Locations around the city are frequently used for filming or still photography, and residents are accustomed to seeing familiar places like the pier, the Third Street Promenade, and local restaurants appear in movies and television shows. In 2002, an estimated 800 permits were issued by the city for filming or still photography. In addition, Santa Monica hosts entertainment industry events, such as the annual American Film Market, which brings people from all over the world here to preview and buy films for their hometown theatres. In these ways, Santa Monica plays a significant role in a business with worldwide influence. Since the 1920s, when Hollywood greats colonized the "Gold Coast" on the beach in Santa Monica, the city has been linked to the glamour of Hollywood. Today that connection lives on, not only because many stars and celebrities still choose to live here, but because the city itself is now a player in the business of making entertainment.

Santa Monica

Tourism and leisure, the economic engines that have evolved over time but remain central to Santa Monica's livelihood, are another link to the past. Just as Santa Monica's city fathers aimed at attracting "high-class" tourists a century ago, the city today works to attract upscale visitors as a mainstay of the city's economy. However, where bathhouses, drinking, or dancing on the pier once attracted fun-seekers, today shopping is the leisure activity that brings in the crowds. As described earlier, Santa Monica's civic leaders remade Third Street into the pedestrian-friendly and popular Santa Monica Mall in the 1960s. In the early 1980s shopping opportunities were enhanced by the opening of Santa Monica Place, the indoor mall across from Sears. But keeping this area vital has required continued tinkering by the city. By the time Santa Monica Place opened, Santa Monica Mall appeared to be "running downhill."[107] Indeed, in a cyclical pattern of revival and decay that will seem familiar to downtown watchers, by the late 1970s the Mall was considered seedy and city officials and local businesspeople concluded it was no longer attracting higher-end shoppers. The response was another facelift for Third Street. What emerged was the Third Street Promenade, which encompassed the old Mall but extended pedestrian-only traffic all the way from Wilshire Boulevard to Santa Monica Place at Broadway. Studded with several multi-screen movie theatres, numerous restaurants, bookstores, many national chain stores, and street performers, the Promenade today draws huge crowds, especially on weekends. Indeed, the Promenade and other businesses and restaurants in the downtown area are so popular that nearby streets and freeway off-ramps are frequently jammed with carloads of people just trying to get there. Although in 2004 some analysts warned that the city was "losing its edge" as a shopping destination (to newer developments such as The Grove in Los Angeles), for the moment visitors with money to spend keep coming.[108]

Beyond shopping, Santa Monica also attracts many well-to-do tourists to its hotels, including several expensive new establishments on the beach south of the Santa Monica Pier. In 1989 Loews Santa Monica Beach Hotel opened at 1700 Ocean Avenue, billing itself as "Los Angeles's only luxury beachfront hotel."[109] It did not hold this distinction long, however, because several other posh hotels soon opened nearby, including Shutters-on-the-Beach and the former Casa del Mar beach club, renovated at a cost of $50 million and renamed Hotel Casa del Mar. The terrorist attacks of September 11, 2001, caused a downturn in tourism in Santa Monica, especially from international visitors, but the hotel industry in the city is generally healthy. The fact that the average room rate in Santa Monica today is more than $200 per night affirms that the city's long-standing strategy of appealing to well-heeled visitors is working. Thus, while many of Santa Monica's luxurious hotels are new, they are part of a much older tradition, begun in the nineteenth century when places like the Arcadia Hotel were first built, to serve a discriminating clientele.

Luckily for more ordinary folks wanting to enjoy Santa Monica, not all amusements are so exclusive. The city's beaches are open to people from all walks of life, just as they have been from the earliest days of settlement, and summer weekends still bring thousands of Angelinos seeking relief from inland heat. The old-fashioned charms of Santa Monica Pier are equally egalitarian. The pier was fully purchased by the city in 1974, badly damaged by violent winter storms in 1983, and then restored under the auspices of the non-profit Pier Restoration Corporation. Today the pier attracts tourists and residents alike to its carousel, arcade games, and Pacific Park amusement area featuring rides, a roller coaster, and a Ferris wheel. Restaurants, small shops, fishing, and special events such as the Twilight Dance series also bring people to the pier. A small aquarium under the pier, operated by Heal the Bay, offers an educational look into Santa Monica Bay's marine ecology. And for the informed observer, the view from the pier reveals a fascinating panoply of reminders from the city's past. From the still-pristine Santa Monica Mountains toward Malibu that are not much altered from when the Gabrielino knew them, to the remnants of the old breakwater rising from the tide, to vestiges of Marion Davies's Gold Coast estate up the beach, to the high-rises of the mid-twentieth century, to the playground that was Muscle Beach—the pier offers the quiet satisfaction of connecting with Santa Monica's history. Whether in fancy hotels or in such simple pleasures, Santa Monica's 150-year-old tradition of tourism and leisure lives on today and remains a key component of the city's prosperity.

The tradition of sports innovation that has woven through Santa Monica's history has also continued into the recent past. We have already seen how cutting-edge Santa Monicans poured their energy into tennis, road racing, and bodybuilding, and had a lasting impact on these endeavors. The most recent efflorescence of this innovative impulse has been in a sport with a grittier, more urban edge—skateboarding. A recent documentary film by Stacy Peralta, *Dogtown and Z-Boys*, relates the story of how a group of gifted athletes from the south side of Santa Monica and Venice revolutionized skateboarding in the 1970s. These young men and women—including now legendary figures such as Peralta, Jay Adams, and Tony Alva—applied the aesthetics and techniques of surfing to the street, using skateboards in ways never seen before. As the Zephyr Team, organized around an Ocean Park surf shop, they dominated the nation's first major skateboarding competition in 1975. Then, capitalizing on the drought that forced many local homeowners to drain their swimming pools in the mid-1970s, they pioneered vertical skateboarding. As reporter Sal Ruibal wrote:

> The pools turned out to be the perfect medium for the sport. Alva and Adams were especially adept at making pivot turns closer and closer to the top edge of the pool. One day, no one remembers the exact date or place, the eureka moment arrived. Alva pushed higher and higher until his vertical board cleared the edge of the pool and he was no longer riding on Earth. From that point on, tricks on skateboards, and later snowboards, wakeboards and BMX bikes would be performed in midair.[110]

The influence of these pioneers endures in the continued popular interest in skateboarding, the existence of many professionally-organized competitions, and the growth of "extreme" sports of all kinds. Where new innovations in sport will blossom next is a mystery, but judging from past experience, there is a good chance that the cutting edge will be in Santa Monica.

If what people do here has both changed and remained the same, so have the people themselves. Santa Monica has always been a place where diverse people have made important contributions to the city's well-being, and this remains true today. Beginning in the earliest days the Gabrielino, Spanish, and Mexicans all played a role in shaping Santa Monica. After American rule began, many other groups appeared on the scene including African Americans, Chinese, and Japanese, to name just a few. But as times have changed, the city's mix of people has too. Today Santa Monica is predominantly white, but with significant exceptions. In the year 2003 some 72 percent of the city's residents were caucasian. Still, 4 percent of the population is African American, 13 percent is Hispanic, and 7 percent is Asian. With these percentages, Santa Monica has proportionately fewer African Americans, Hispanics, and Asians than surrounding Los Angeles. However, at the same time Santa Monica is less white than it has been in the recent past. In 1980, for example, whites made up 78 percent of the population, 6 percent more than today.

These numbers represent shifts in the concentration of racial and ethnic minorities that have long played a role in local history. Santa Monica's black community has lost numbers steadily in the last few decades. In 1970 some 4,041 African Americans resided here. By the year 2000 the number had dropped to 3,176. The number of Hispanic residents, by contrast, has increased from 10,668 in 1970 to 11,304 as of 2000. (Diversity can now be found throughout the city. Still, many blacks and Hispanics continue to reside in the Pico Neighborhood, as has been true in the past, and it remains the city's most racially diverse area.) Meanwhile, other groups formerly absent have found a place in Santa Monica. Persians, for example, are a relatively new group in in the city, but one that has increased in visibility since heavy migration from Iran began in the 1970s. The reasons for these changes are complex and how these trends will play out in the twenty-first century remains to be seen. What is clear, however, is that just as African-American, Hispanic, Asian, and Native-American people have contributed to the city's past in numerous vital ways, diverse groups will continue to enrich the city's future.

These recent trends in Santa Monica's history tell us something about the city today. But there have been other profound developments at work at the same time. The story of how "radical" political activism has reshaped the city in recent decades is a particularly important one. However, another trend—towards gentrification—has had an equally important effect on the city. Needless to say, progressive politics and gentrification do not always mesh well. Indeed, the tension and interplay between left-leaning politics and a city that is growing ever richer and more exclusive has created conflict and competing visions of what the city should be.

To the Present

The story of progressive politics picks up where we left off at the end of Chapter Nine. That chapter ended with a description of how, in the 1970s, pro-development forces were reined in as citizens and grassroots organizations battled to curtail coastal development and preserve the Santa Monica Pier. Indeed, the unbridled development of mid-century, described in the last chapter, served as a prologue for new political forces that emerged in the late 1970s and early 1980s to rewrite the rules of how the city was run. These forces, which coalesced into an organization known as Santa Monicans for Renters' Rights (SMRR), eventually gained control of city hall and brought the city to the cutting edge on a whole host of progressive issues. For more than twenty years, and continuing to the present day, voters have supported these left-leaning activists.

The emergence of an effective leftist alternative to the development ethic that has historically held sway in Southern California is one of the most interesting facets of recent local history. The battle to save the pier was an early manifestation of this alternative approach—one that blossomed as Santa Monicans began to realize that the pier was but a small part of larger issues facing the city. Indeed, through the 1970s, as people continued to stream into Southern California and real estate in desirable areas like Santa Monica was in increasingly high demand, a sense that the city's very integrity was at stake grew among residents and activists. Citizens succeeded in preserving the pier—a potent symbol—but development and growth still seemed to threaten the quality of life many residents had come to appreciate. The destruction or conversion of many apartment buildings to make way for high-priced condominiums, along with skyrocketing rents on the apartments that remained, particularly disturbed many Santa Monicans.

By 1978, SMRR, a grassroots organization aimed at slowing these trends, had coalesced, driven by activists schooled in the radical movements of the 1960s. In 1979, due in large part to the organizing efforts of SMRR members, whose ideas struck a nerve among many Santa Monicans, voters agreed to amend the city charter to establish rent control in Santa Monica, along with a rent control board to enforce it. The new law—one of the toughest in the nation—was intended to preserve low and moderate income rental housing in the city, control rents on residential units, and limit the circumstances in which landlords could evict tenants while, it was hoped, still encouraging landlords to maintain their properties.

The passage of rent control in Santa Monica was a remarkable fact in itself and heralded a new approach to how Santa Monica would be managed. But this was far from the end of left-leaning politics in Santa Monica. Indeed, influenced in part by the work of well-known activist Tom Hayden and his Campaign for Economic Democracy and other progressive movements of the time, a new generation of leaders associated with SMRR, including Dennis Zane, Dolores Press, Kenneth Edwards, Ruth Yannatta Goldway, and Derek Shearer, were gaining support among Santa Monicans and would soon reshape local politics more generally. By 1981, building on gains made in the late 1970s, SMRR candidates won control of the city council for the first time, capturing five of seven seats. A new era of SMRR dominance had begun. Over only a couple of years, thanks to energetic leadership and well-coordinated campaigns, SMRR had evolved from a small, informal coalition into a formidable political force with thousands of supporters.

In a sense, the success of leftist activism in Santa Monica was a surprising turn of events. After all, as recently as 1964, Santa Monica had been a largely Republican town. (In 1962, gubernatorial hopeful Richard Nixon won easily in Santa Monica.) However, it is also true that by the 1970s, when SMRR was founded, Santa Monica—like California generally—was a place where people with alternative ideas about how society could work were both attracted and nurtured. Moreover, Southern California has long had a reputation for being a place where new social and political movements find fertile soil.

Whatever its roots, Santa Monica, which had been famous for many things over the years, now achieved widespread notoriety for its "radical" politics. The city and its mediagenic new leaders were featured on CBS's "60 Minutes" program, in national magazines, and in newspapers across the country as SMRR worked to flesh out a program for the city that would go beyond just rent control. Looking at the first few years of city governance under SMRR, historian Mark Kann identified three core concerns of the evolving SMRR program. First was a preference for preserving a "human scale" city, rather than one in which development and growth would strip away the character and quality of life in the city. Second was a desire to encourage participatory democracy. And third was a preference for economic democracy in which, for example, landlords could not wring "excessive" profits from tenants, and small businesses were favored over large corporations.[111] Whether one agrees with these basic ideas or not, and whether or not SMRR itself has remained true to them, have been subjects of much debate. However, whatever one's views, there is no doubt that these general ideals have played out in a variety of city programs and policies in the last two and a half decades and marked Santa Monica as an innovator.

Rent control, naturally, has been the centerpiece of the SMRR program and the organization's long-standing commitment to it has meant that today there are some 30,000 rent-controlled housing units in Santa Monica, allowing some lower-income residents to remain in the city who might otherwise have been forced to move because of rising rents. (It must be noted, however, that many tenants enjoying rent-controlled rates are not low-income.) Lower-income residents have also been aided by the city's commitment to building additional affordable housing throughout the city. In 2004, for example, Mayor Richard Bloom estimated that the city produces about 156 units of affordable housing per year. SMRR has been proud of these efforts to maintain the city's economic diversity. Yet it must be noted that recently Santa Monica's strict rent control laws have been altered to conform to state regulations with the effect that landlords can now raise rents on vacated units to market rates. The result is that rents, even on rent-controlled units, can be much higher than previously allowed. Another recent change to rent control, in which tenants who do not occupy their units full-time may forfeit their rent-controlled rates, has also weakened the city's strict standards. Nonetheless, SMRR today remains committed to the principle of rent control and celebrated the twenty-fifth anniversary of the city's path-breaking law, a turning point in the city's history, in April of 2004.

Aside from rent control, SMRR has generally enacted much stricter controls on development than had existed before, and continues to do so today. While residents and developers do not always agree with the process the city uses to arrive at decisions, there is no question that the days when developers could expect the city to rubber stamp their projects are long gone. Under the guidance of SMRR leaders, the city has also worked to protect unique and historic structures in the city. Spurred by the city's centennial celebrations, a landmarks commission was formed in 1976 that instituted formal procedures for identifying and designating historical landmarks in the city. In the same year, the Santa Monica Pier and its carousel were among the city's first designated landmarks. Since then some fifty-three historic sites have been accorded landmark status. These include public buildings such as City Hall, apartment buildings including the Charmont Apartments at 330 California Street, theatres such as the Mayfair on Santa Monica Boulevard near Second Street, private homes of many architectural styles, and notable trees. In addition, the Third Street Neighborhood Historic District in Ocean Park, consisting of thirty-eight buildings, is the city's first protected historic district. These efforts to safeguard historic structures and educate the public about the city's past are augmented by the work of the Santa Monica Conservancy, a volunteer organization founded in 2002.

SMRR's sense of stewardship has also included an emphasis on "sustainability," in which environmentalism has played a significant role in how the city operates. Indeed, an ambitious Sustainable City Plan, adopted by the city in 1994, states that "City decision-making will be guided by a mandate to maximize environmental benefits and reduce or eliminate negative environmental impacts." In line with this plan, the city currently purchases "green" power generated from environmentally-friendly sources, has implemented an extensive recycling program, helps organize citizens to learn more about sustainable practices, and gives out "Sustainability Awards" to notable businesses and organizations that make Santa Monica a cleaner more livable place. The wide-ranging Sustainable City Plan also aims at increasing the construction of "green" buildings, improving air quality, promoting the health of Santa Monica Bay, encouraging the use of locally-grown organic produce, reducing excessive water use, lowering greenhouse gas emissions, and reducing solid-waste generation, among other things. Recently, the city has also worked to increase the use of public transportation by building a transit mall downtown and made life easier for pedestrians and bicyclists by improving traffic signals, crosswalks, and bike lanes around the city.

Yet even as the powers in city hall strive to keep Santa Monica "livable," working to make it possible for people of different economic levels to reside here, praising small businesses, and stressing the importance of preserving the city's unique heritage, the powerful forces of gentrification often work in the opposite direction. No one knows how far gentrification will go, but there is no doubt that it is changing both the city and its people, creating new tensions and intensifying the long-running debate about what Santa Monica should be.

Ever since the first lots in Santa Monica were auctioned off in 1875, the city's fortunes have been charted in its land prices. In Southern California, alternating booms and busts in real estate have seemed as natural as breathing, but the trend over time has been toward higher prices as more and more people have migrated to the region looking for the good life. In the decades after the city's founding, of course, higher prices were welcomed as evidence of a thriving community. Rising land prices offered reassurance that Santa Monica would not become a ghost town like some other upstart towns in the region. However, too much of a good thing can cause problems. In recent years Santa Monica, with its particularly favorable location, easy access to Los Angeles, desirable quality of life, and exemplary public schools, has seen the costs of owning property explode. With virtually no open land to develop and relatively tight controls on building, there is simply not enough space for all who wish to live here. Santa Monica is already more densely populated than Los Angeles. Thus, in various parts of the city today it is quite common to see small, poorly-maintained bungalows on modest lots sell for well over a million dollars. The houses themselves are not worth much and are often torn down, to be replaced by mini-mansions squeezed onto the precious land. Condominiums too have seen dramatic increases in value in the last few years. And even neighborhoods that have been less subject to gentrification in recent years, such as Sunset Park, are now attracting more attention as buyers find homes there—which at the moment start in the low-$700,000—a relative "bargain."

This trend toward extremely expensive real estate has had and will continue to have important consequences for the city. The economic diversity that marked Santa Monica in the mid-twentieth century, and what the city's leaders have attempted to preserve, is fast eroding. Indeed, hand-in-hand with changes in real estate prices have gone changes in the city's residents, which today number about 86,000. Writing in the mid-1980s, historian Mark Kann already perceived a shift from Santa Monica as a small all-American city "with a population mix representative of the nation," to the city's "new status of being an in-town suburb for the well-to-do."[112]

This shift only accelerated in the 1990s. Between 1990 and 2000, the median household income for Santa Monica rose by a startling 41 percent, and a city report noted that the number of households with income over $150,000 per year had doubled. The average yearly household income in 2000 was just shy of $80,000. Without a doubt, residents of Santa Monica today are generally wealthier than residents of Los Angeles, and they are better educated too. More than half of all Santa Monicans over the age of twenty-five have a bachelor's degree or higher, while only about a quarter of Los Angeles County adults have reached these goals. Not surprisingly, a full 60 percent of employed Santa Monicans work in management, professional, or related occupations, and this figure is expected to continue rising. A large percentage of the remaining residents do sales or office work. Unlike in the past, very few Santa Monicans today can be called "blue-collar" workers. Rather, Santa Monicans today are, generally speaking, a privileged group, and are becoming more so every day as less privileged people are increasingly priced out of the city.

It is not only lower-income people who are finding Santa Monica impossible to afford. As the city has become increasingly upscale, local businesses with deep roots in the community are also being forced out. Recently, for example, Santa Monicans were dismayed to hear that the last lumber yard in the city, Fisher Lumber, will close because the land it occupies at Fourteenth and Colorado is just too valuable to use for selling wood and hardware. Polly's Café, an unpretentious neighborhood hangout at Wilshire and Fifth Street, served its last pie and coffee in March of 2004 because the diner could no longer afford the downtown area. Meanwhile, the Third Street Promenade has been so successful in attracting shoppers that rents on retail properties there have skyrocketed, pushing out small, locally-owned businesses and opening the way for a profusion of chain stores. The Midnight Special bookstore, for decades a resource and gathering place for independent-minded people, was one casualty. A rent hike forced it off the Promenade and the costs of moving to a new location were fatal. It closed in June of 2004.

These changes have elicited a variety of reactions from Santa Monicans, many of them negative. Some, such as resident Connie Cole, lament that the city has "become like everywhere else, more cookie-cutter. . . . The middle class is being pushed out."[113] Others decry the loss of "our sense of place."[114] Along these same lines a recent letter to the *Santa Monica Mirror* bewailed the fact that "the old, real Santa Monica . . . is being chipped away in a persistent and unrelenting fashion, leaving in its wake the homogenized and sanitized landscape of upscale coffee shops, boutiques, and high end office space."[115] Even those areas, like Main Street in Ocean Park, that have not yet been overrun in this way seem, to many residents, "vulnerable, at any time, to flipping right into the plastic mall-dom the way the Promenade did."[116] Some, such as Vivian Rothstein, long active in progressive causes in the city, describe recent trends in even darker terms: "It's like this monster that's trying to take us over," she says. Overall, a *Los Angeles Times* article on the city reported, "a sense of unease, even guilt, that hangs over the place, as if some people are debating whether Santa Monica should be sister city to Brentwood or Berkeley."[117]

Having held the reins of power in Santa Monica for more than two decades, SMRR is often blamed for gentrification and its side effects. It is true that the city's decisions have, in some ways, contributed to rising real estate prices, traffic problems, and other ills. For example, by favoring the development of an expensive hotel district along the beach in the 1990s, city leaders naturally encouraged wealthy tourists to visit, creating greater demand for upscale shopping, dining, and leisure activities.

Santa Monica

By promoting the Third Street Promenade heavily and encouraging visitors from all over the region and the world to visit it, traffic has worsened and the demand for retail space shot up along with prices. Similarly, the tendency to favor development of high-end office space as a land use with relatively low environmental impacts, has, predictably, attracted high-end users of such space to the city generally. However, as much as people like to blame SMRR for undesirable changes in the city, it is not hard to envision a city leadership that would have hastened these changes along much more quickly. Moreover, it must be remarked that the high level of activist programs and services the city provides, which few Santa Monicans seem to wish to see reduced (from programs to promote the arts, to preservation, to affordable housing, to environmental efforts, to pier maintenance, to support of the public schools), would not be possible without the revenues that the city earns from the tourist industry, retail sector, and office developments. Indeed, the very success of Santa Monica as a progressive experiment is predicated on a city budget more bountiful than that of many cities of comparable size.

Aside from this, the fact is that Santa Monica is not an island. Many of the things residents perceive as negative stem from regional trends largely out of the control of city government. For example, the number of people moving to the Southland is growing by leaps and bounds. Figures released in 2004 show that a million newcomers relocated to Southern California in the last three years alone. In addition, over recent decades population in the Los Angeles area has been concentrating increasingly on the west side. Over the course of Santa Monica's history, the city has become ever more intimately entwined with the greater Los Angeles metropolis and these days thousands upon thousands of people cross in and out of Santa Monica every day. The fact that in the year 2000 more than two-thirds of Santa Monicans reported holding jobs outside the city begins to suggest the level of fluidity between Santa Monica and neighboring cities. With urbanized Los Angeles encircling Santa Monica, it would be naïve to expect that traffic levels and congestion could remain low here when they are rising in surrounding areas. Similarly, real estate prices throughout Southern California have been on the upswing for quite some time and no area can be insulated from this, short of a change to radical government on a much wider scale.

However, the fact that issues affecting Santa Monica have complex causes does not necessarily diminish conflict here. On the contrary, Santa Monica at present is a city rife with impassioned debates and, from a historical perspective, this is not unexpected. Santa Monica today has come a long way from what it was at its founding in 1875, and even further from the place Mexican and Spanish settlers and native Gabrielinos once knew. But from then until now one question has remained salient: What will Santa Monica be? Moreover, from its earliest days when Senator Jones decided to defy the powerful railroad interests and do things his own way, to when Santa Monicans decided to buck Los Angeles in the 1920s and retain their independence, to the present day, both the city and its residents have proven that an independent spirit is a local trait that will continue to shape Santa Monica's destiny into the future.

A great many of the debates going on in Santa Monica inspire passionate opinions and high emotions precisely because they touch on deep questions of the city's identity, values, and future. For one, how much development and of what kind is right for Santa Monica? As the city weighs proposals to modify the downtown area in 2004, there will be a delicate line to walk that somehow allows for change without overwhelming what makes the city unique and special.

Equally important, will Santa Monica's changing, and increasingly upscale population, continue to support the progressive causes that have made Santa Monica so distinctive in recent decades? Should the city continue its efforts to make Santa Monica accessible to a wide range of people or should, as some propose, the market alone determine who will enjoy Santa Monica in the future? Answers to these questions will determine the long-term future of programs like rent control. The city's large homeless population—currently the subject of fiery debate—will offer an extreme test of how inclusive Santa Monicans are willing to be.

How to create a balance between livability for residents and attractiveness to tourists and newcomers is another challenge. There are advantages to Santa Monica when people from all over the region, and indeed the world, flock here for entertainment and the good life, but disadvantages as well if congestion and high prices destroy what people found so attractive here in the first place.

Looming over these questions is a larger issue: To what extent can Santa Monica determine its own destiny in the twenty-first century when it is, undeniably, a small city surrounded by a much larger metropolis that is itself part of a dynamic and changing region?

Only time will tell what direction Santa Monica will take in the future. But if the past is any guide, expect Santa Monica to keep its edge and continue making interesting history.

NOTES

Chapter One

1. Eargle, Dolan H. Jr. *The Earth is our Mother*. San Francisco: Trees Company Press, 1986, xv.

Chapter Two

2. McCawley, William. *The First Angelinos: The Gabrielino Indians of Los Angeles*. Banning, CA: Malki Museum Press/Ballena Press, 1996, 4.
3. Weber, David J. *The Spanish Frontier in North America*. New Haven: Yale University Press, 1992, 41.
4. Costansó, Miguel. *The Discovery of San Francisco Bay: The Portolá Expedition of 1769–1770*. Peter Browning, ed. Lafayette, CA: Great West Books, 1992, 21.
5. Crespí, Fray Juan. *Fray Juan Crespí, Missionary Explorer on the Pacific Coast*. Herbert Eugene Bolton, ed. Berkeley: University of California Press, 1927, 149–150.
6. Browning, ed. *The Discovery of San Francisco Bay: The Portolá Expedition of 1769–1770*, 23.
7. Heizer, Robert F., ed. *The Indians of Los Angeles County: Hugo Reid's Letters of 1852*. Los Angeles: Southwest Museum, 1968, 69.
8. Weber. *The Spanish Frontier in North America*, 12.
9. Englehardt, Zephyrin. *San Gabriel Mission and the Beginnings of Los Angeles*. San Gabriel, CA: Mission San Gabriel, 1927, 101.
10. Englehardt. *San Gabriel Mission and the Beginnings of Los Angeles*, 59.

Chapter Three

11. Weber, David J. *The Spanish Frontier in North America*. New Haven: Yale University Press, 1992, 264.
12. Webb, Edith Buckland. *Indian Life at the Old Missions*. Lincoln, NE: University of Nebraska Press, 1982, 294.
13. *California Ranchos: Fact Cards*. Milpitas, CA: Toucan Valley Publications, 1997, card 9.
14. Englehardt, Zephyrin. *San Gabriel Mission and the Beginnings of Los Angeles*. San Gabriel, CA: Mission San Gabriel, 1927, 62–63.
15. Wilson, Benjamin Davis. *The Indians of Southern California in 1852*. John W. Caughey, ed. San Marino, CA: Huntington Library, 1952, 21.
16. Warren, Charles S., ed. *Santa Monica Community Book*. Santa Monica: Arthur H. Cawston, 1944, 99.
17. Warren. *Santa Monica Community Book*, 98.
18. Beasley, Delilah L. *Negro Trailblazers of California*. San Francisco: California Historical Society & San Francisco Negro Historical and Cultural Society, 1968, 90.
19. Stern, Norton B. "Jews in Early Santa Monica: A Centennial Review." *Western States Jewish Historical Quarterly* (July 1975), 2.
20. Waitt, Helen and Mary Collier Wayne, eds. *We Three Came West: A True Chronicle*. San Diego: Tofua Press, 1974, 152–153.

Chapter Four

21. *Figaro*, July 9, 1875 in Ernest Marquez, *Port Los Angeles: A Phenomenon of the Railroad Era*.

San Marino, CA: Golden West Books, 1975, 8.

22. McWilliams, Carey. *Southern California Country: An Island on the Land*. New York: Duell, Sloan & Pearce, 1946, 116.

23. *Los Angeles Daily Star*, July 16, 1875, quoted in Norton B. Stern, "Jews in Early Santa Monica: A Centennial Review." *Western States Jewish Historical Quarterly* (July 1975), 1.

24. McWilliams. *Southern California Country: An Island on the Land*, 124.

25. Wolf, Marvin J. and Katherine Mader. *Santa Monica: Jewel of the Sunset Bay*. Chatsworth, CA: Windsor Publishing, 1989, 19.

26. *Outlook*. Nov. 24, 1875.

27. Marquez, Ernest. *Port Los Angeles: A Phenomenon of the Railroad Era*, xii.

28. *New York World*, June 26, 1894, quoted in Marquez, *Port Los Angeles: A Phenomenon of the Railroad Era*, 70.

Chapter Five

29. Warren, Charles S. *Santa Monica Community Book*. Santa Monica: Arthur H. Cawston, 1944, 21.

30. Stern, Norton B. "Jews of Early Santa Monica: A Centennial Review." *Western States Jewish Historical Quarterly* (July 1975), 14.

31. Warren. *Santa Monica Community Book*, 94.

32. McWilliams, Carey. *Southern California Country: An Island on the Land*. New York: Duell, Sloan & Pearce, 1946, 151.

33. McWilliams. *Southern California Country: An Island on the Land*, 151.

34. "SM's Original Families Suffer Discrimination." *Evening Outlook*, May 17, 1975.

35. "Passing of Notable Woman." *Daily Outlook*, Sept. 16, 1912.

36. "SM Blacks Develop Own Culture." *Evening Outlook*, May 17, 1975.

37. "SM Retailers Outgrow Village Image, Confront New Problems." *Evening Outlook*, May 17, 1975.

38. McWilliams. *Southern California Country: An Island on the Land*, 85.

39. Marquez, Ernest. *Port Los Angeles: A Phenomenon of the Railroad Era*. San Marino, CA: Golden West Books, 1975, 98.

40. Stern, Norton B. "Jews of Early Santa Monica: A Centennial Review." *Western States Jewish Historical Quarterly* (July 1975), 4.

41. McWilliams. *Southern California Country: An Island on the Land*, 41.

42. *Los Angeles Star*, Aug. 22, 1876, quoted in Stern, "Jews in Early Santa Monica: A Centennial Review," 6.

43. "SM Blacks Develop Own Culture," *Evening Outlook*, May 17, 1975.

Chapter Six

44. *Los Angeles Times* quoted in Harold L. Osmer and Phil Harms, *Real Road Racing: The Santa Monica Road Races*. Chatsworth, CA: Harold L. Osmer Publishing, 1999, 29.

45. Raitt, Helen. and Mary Collier Wayne, eds. *We Three Came West: A True Chronicle*. San Diego: Tofua Press, 1974, 151–153.

46. Advertisement for North Beach Bathhouse. *Outlook*, Apr. 22, 1893.

47. Stern, Norton B. "Jews of Early Santa Monica: A Centennial Review." *Western States Jewish Historical Quarterly* (July 1975), 11.

48. *Outlook*, Mar. 10, 1899 quoted in "Historic District Application for Third Street Neighborhood in Ocean Park" Vol. II. Santa Monica: 1990, 33.

49. Murphy, Thomas D. *On Sunset Highways: A Book of Motor Rambles in California*. Boston: L.C. Page and Co., 1922, 21.

50. Stanton, Jeffrey. *Santa Monica Pier: A History from 1875 to 1990*. Los Angeles: Donahue Publishing, 1990, 35.

51. Stanton. *Santa Monica Pier: A History from 1875 to 1990*, 29.

52. "Marion Davies' Beach House Becomes Hotel." *Los Angeles Examiner*, Oct. 16, 1949.

53. Warren, Charles S. *Santa Monica Blue Book: Historical and Biographical*. Santa Monica: Arthur H. Cawston, 1941, 134.

54. McWilliams, Carey. *Southern California Country: An Island on the Land*. New York: Duell, Sloan and Pearce, 1946, 110.

55. *Outlook* quoted in Osmer and Harms, *Real Road Racing: The Santa Monica Road Races*, 21.

56. *Motor Age* quoted in Osmer and Harms, *Real Road Racing: The Santa Monica Road Races*, 25.

57. *Los Angeles Times* quoted in Osmer and Harms, *Real Road Racing: The Santa Monica Road Races*, 37.

58. Warren. Charles S. *Santa Monica Community Book*. Santa Monica: Arthur H. Cawston, 1944, 100.

59. Wolf, Marvin J. and Katherine Mader. *Santa Monica: Jewel of the Sunset Bay*. Northridge, CA: Windsor Publishing, 1989, 41.

60. Wolf and Mader. *Santa Monica: Jewel of the Sunset Bay*, 41.

61. Starr, Kevin. *Material Dreams: Southern California through the 1920s*. New York: Oxford University Press, 1990, 60.

62. Starr, Kevin. *The Dream Endures: California Enters the 1940s*. New York: Oxford University Press, 1997, 159.

63. "City Almost Washed Out in Great '24 Water War." *Evening Outlook*, May 17, 1975.

Chapter Seven

64. Author interview with Lloyd Allen. June 2, 2003.

65. "SM's Original Families Suffer Discrimination." *Evening Outlook*, May 17, 1975.

66. Chandler, Raymond. *Farewell, My Lovely*. New York: Vintage Books, 1976, 159.

67. Warren, Charles S. *Santa Monica Blue Book: Historical and Biographical*. Santa Monica: Arthur H. Cawston, 1941, 35.

68. "Tragedy Born Aboard Cornero's Game Vessel Echoed in Court Case." *Evening Outlook*, Aug. 8, 1939.

69. "Cornero Says Rex May be Reopened." *Evening Outlook*, Aug. 4, 1939.

70. "Cornero and Gunmen Continue Defiance as All Ship Gambling Halted." *Evening Outlook*, Aug. 3, 1939.

71. "Bid for Gambling Old Story to SM." *Evening Outlook*, June 17, 1964.

72. McGroarty, John Steven. *California of the South: A History*. Vol. I. Chicago: S.J. Clarke Publishing Co., 1933, 451.

73. Zinkin, Harold with Bonnie Hearn. *Remembering Muscle Beach: Where Hard Bodies Began*. Santa Monica: Angel City Press, 1999, 17, 10.

74. Rose, Marla Matzer. *Muscle Beach*. New York: St. Martin's Griffin, 2001, 68.

75. Zinkin. *Remembering Muscle Beach: Where Hard Bodies Began*, 57.

Chapter Eight

76. Warren, Charles S. *Santa Monica Community Book*. Santa Monica: Arthur H. Cawston, 1944, 107.

77. Starr, Kevin. *Embattled Dreams: California in War and Peace, 1940–1950*. New York: Oxford University Press, 2002, 36.

78. Blakemore, Dana Lyn. *From Settlement to Resettlement: Japanese-Americans in (and out of) Santa Monica, California, 1899–1960*. Ann Arbor, MI: UMI Dissertation Services, 2001, 59.

79. Blakemore. *From Settlement to Resettlement: Japanese-Americans in (and out of) Santa Monica, California, 1899–1960*, 73.

80. "And Prepares Itself for the Furies of War." *Evening Outlook*, May 17, 1975.

81. Blakemore. *From Settlement to Resettlement: Japanese-Americans in (and out of) Santa Monica, California, 1899–1960*, 64.

Notes

82. Starr. *Embattled Dreams: California in War and Peace, 1940–1950*, 135.

83. *Fortune*, March 1943, quoted in Arthur C. Verge, *Paradise Transformed: Los Angeles during the Second World War*. Dubuque, IA: Kendall/Hunt Publishing Co., 1993, 49.

84. Terkel, Studs. *The Good War: An Oral History of World War II*. New York: Pantheon Books, 1984, 116.

85. Warren. *Santa Monica Community Book*, 102.

86. Verge. *Paradise Transformed: Los Angeles during the Second World War*, 116.

87. Verge. *Paradise Transformed: Los Angeles during the Second World War*, 72.

Chapter Nine

88. "Civic Leaders Launch Veteran Housing Action." *Evening Outlook*, Jan. 17, 1946.

89. Blakemore, Dana Lyn. *From Settlement to Resettlement: Japanese-Americans in (and out of) Santa Monica, California, 1899–1960*. Ann Arbor, MI: UMI Dissertation Service, 2001, 133.

90. "SM Government Evolves as City Grows." *Evening Outlook*, May 17, 1975.

91. City of Santa Monica. "Annual Report, 1951–1952."

92. Storrs, Les. *Santa Monica: Portrait of a City, Yesterday and Today*. Santa Monica: Santa Monica Bank, 1974, 44.

93. "Sleepy SM Leaps on Industrial Bandwagon." *Evening Outlook*, May 17, 1975.

94. "SM Mall: More than a Facelift." *Evening Outlook*, May 17, 1975.

95. City of Santa Monica. "Annual Report, 1968–1969."

96. Storrs. *Santa Monica: Portrait of a City, Yesterday and Today*, 54.

97. "SM Freeway Links LA with Bay Communities." *Evening Outlook*, May 17, 1975.

98. "Freeway Splits Minority Neighborhood." *Evening Outlook*, May 17, 1975.

99. "Freeway Runs Through Sore Spot." *Evening Outlook*, Apr. 24, 1964.

100. "Freeway Splits Minority Neighborhood." *Evening Outlook*, May 17, 1975.

101. Blakemore. *From Settlement to Resettlement: Japanese-Americans in (and out of) Santa Monica, California, 1899–1960*, 194.

102. City of Santa Monica. "Annual Report, 1966–1967."

103. "SM Freeway Links LA with Bay Communities." *Evening Outlook*, May 17, 1975.

104. Stanton, Jeffrey. *Santa Monica Pier: A History from 1875 to 1990*. Los Angeles: Donahue Publishing, 1990, 132.

105. "Construction of PCH: Digging in for a Battle." *Evening Outlook*, May 17, 1975.

106. Stanton. *Santa Monica Pier: A History from 1875 to 1990*, 138.

Chapter Ten

107. "SM Retailers Outgrow Village Image, Confront New Problems." *Evening Outlook*, May 17, 1975.

108. "City Loses Competitive Edge, According to Leading Economist." *Santa Monica Mirror*, Jan. 14–20, 2004.

109. "Invitation." Loews Santa Monica Beach Hotel, June 23, 1989.

110. "Cutting-edge sports trace roots back to 1970s." *USA Today*, April 17, 2002.

111. Kann, Mark E. *Middle Class Radicalism in Santa Monica*. Philadelphia: Temple University Press, 1986, chap. 3.

112. Kann. *Middle Class Radicalism in Santa Monica*, 62.

113. "Last Call: Polly's to Close in March." *Santa Monica Mirror*, Feb. 25–Mar. 2, 2004.

114. "When Bureaucrats Dream, They Dream of Deserts." *Santa Monica Mirror*, April 9–15, 2003.

115. "Deploring loss of Fisher." *Santa Monica Mirror*, April 9–15, 2003.

116. "That Main Refrain . . ." *Santa Monica Mirror*, Nov. 19–25, 2003.

117. "Sea Change in Santa Monica." *Los Angeles Times*, Oct. 16, 2002.

BIBLIOGRAPHY

Basten, Fred E. *Santa Monica Bay: Paradise by the Sea*. Los Angeles: General Publishing Group, 1997.

Beck, Warren A. and Ynez D. Haase. *Historical Atlas of California*. Norman, OK: University of Oklahoma Press, 1974.

Blakemore, Dana Lyn. *From Settlement to Resettlement: Japanese-Americans in (and out of) Santa Monica, California, 1899–1960*. Ann Arbor, MI: UMI Dissertation Services, 2001.

Bottles, Scott L. *Los Angeles and the Automobile: The Making of the Modern City*. Berkeley, CA: University of California Press, 1987.

"Centennial Edition." *Evening Outlook*, May 17, 1975.

Costansó, Miguel. *The Discovery of San Francisco Bay: The Portolá Expedition of 1769–1770*. Edited by Peter Browning. Lafayette, CA: Great West Books, 1992.

Englehardt, Zephyrin. *San Gabriel Mission and the Beginnings of Los Angeles*. San Gabriel, CA: Mission San Gabriel, 1927.

Heckman, Marlin L. *Santa Monica in Vintage Postcards*. Charleston, SC: Arcadia Publishing, 2002.

Heizer, Robert F. and Albert B. Elsasser. *The Natural World of the California Indians*. Berkeley, CA: University of California Press, 1980.

Henstell, Bruce. *Sunshine and Wealth: Los Angeles in the Twenties and Thirties*. San Francisco: Chronicle Books, 1984.

"Historic District Application for Third Street Neighborhood in Ocean Park." Santa Monica, July 1990.

Kann, Mark E. *Middle Class Radicalism in Santa Monica*. Philadelphia: Temple University Press, 1986.

Marquez, Ernest. *Port Los Angeles: A Phenomenon of the Railroad Era*. San Marino, CA: Golden West Books, 1975.

McCawley, William. *The First Angelinos: The Gabrielino Indians of Los Angeles*. Banning, CA: Malki Museum Press/Ballena Press, 1996.

McWilliams, Carey. *Southern California Country: An Island on the Land*. New York: Duell, Sloan and Pearce, 1946.

Osmer, Harold L. and Phil Harms. *Real Road Racing: The Santa Monica Road Races*. Chatsworth, CA: Harold L. Osmer Publishing, 1999.

Pearlstone, Zena. *Ethnic L.A.* Beverly Hills, CA: Hillcrest Press, 1990.

Phoenix, Charles. *Southern California in the Fifties*. Santa Monica: Angel City Press, 2001.

Pierson, Robert John. *The Beach Towns: A Walker's Guide to L.A.'s Beach Communities*. San Francisco: Chronicle Books, 1985.

Robinson, W.W. *Los Angeles from the Days of the Pueblo*. San Francisco: California Historical Society, 1959.

Rose, Marla Matzer. *Muscle Beach*. New York: St. Martin's Griffin, 2001.

Santa Monica Landmarks Tour. Santa Monica: City of Santa Monica, Planning Division, 2003.

Bibliography

Stanton, Jeffrey. *Santa Monica Pier: A History from 1875 to 1990*. Los Angeles: Donahue Publishing, 1990.

Starr, Kevin. *Material Dreams: Southern California through the 1920s*. New York: Oxford University Press, 1990.

Starr, Kevin. *Endangered Dreams: The Great Depression in California*. New York: Oxford University Press, 1996.

Starr, Kevin. *The Dream Endures: California enters the 1940s*. New York: Oxford University Press, 1997.

Starr, Kevin. *Embattled Dreams: California in War and Peace, 1940–1950*. New York: Oxford University Press, 2002.

Stern, Norton B. "Jews in Early Santa Monica: A Centennial Review." *Western States Jewish Historical Quarterly*. July 1975.

Storrs, Les. *Santa Monica: Portrait of a City Yesterday and Today*. Santa Monica: Santa Monica Bank, 1974.

Verge, Arthur C. *Paradise Transformed: Los Angeles during the Second World War*. Dubuque, IA: Kendall/Hunt Publishing Co., 1993.

Ward, Elizabeth and Alain Silver. *Raymond Chandler's Los Angeles*. Woodstock, NY: Overlook Press, 1987.

Warren, Charles S., ed. *Santa Monica Blue Book: Historical and Biographical*. Santa Monica: Arthur H. Cawston, 1941.

Warren, Charles S., ed. *Santa Monica Community Book*. Santa Monica: Arthur H. Cawston, 1944.

Webb, Edith Buckland. *Indian Life at the Old Missions*. Lincoln, NE: University of Nebraska Press, 1982.

Weber, David J. *The Spanish Frontier in North America*. New Haven, CT: Yale University Press, 1992.

Wolf, Marvin J. and Katherine Mader. *Santa Monica: Jewel of the Sunset Bay*. Chatsworth, CA: Windsor Publishing, 1989.

Young, Betty Lou and Randy Young. *Santa Monica Canyon: A Walk through History*. Pacific Palisades, CA: Casa Vieja Press, 1997.

Zinkin, Harold with Bonnie Hearn. *Remembering Muscle Beach: Where Hard Bodies Began*. Santa Monica: Angel City Press, 1999.

INDEX

Index